Suicidal Behaviour

of related interest

Suicide
The Tragedy of Hopelessness
David Aldridge
ISBN 1 85302 444 9

Between Therapists
The Processing of Transference/Countertransference Material
Arthur Robbins
ISBN 1 85302 832 0

The Therapist's Encounters with Revenge and Forgiveness
Mary Sherrill Durham
ISBN 1 85302 815 0

Figures of Lightness
Anorexia, Bulimia and Psychoanalysis
Gabriella Ripa di Meana
ISBN 1 85302 617 4

Remorse and Reparation
Edited by Murray Cox
ISBN 1 85302 452 X pb
ISBN 1 85302 451 1 hb

Suicidal Behaviour
A Search for its Psychic Economy

Jürgen Kind

Translated by Paul Foulkes

Jessica Kingsley Publishers
London and Philadelphia

First published in German in 1992 by Vandenhoeck & Ruprecht, Göttingen
First published in the United Kingdom in 1999 by
Jessica Kingsley Publishers Ltd,
116 Pentonville Road, London
N1 9JB, England
and
325 Chestnut Street,
Philadelphia
PA 19106, USA.

www.jkp.com

© Copyright 1992 Vandenhoeck & Ruprecht, Göttingen
© Translation Copyright 1999 Paul Foulkes

Library of Congress Cataloging in Publication Data
A CIP catalog record for this book is available from the Library of Congress

British Library Cataloguing in Publication Data
Kind, Jürgen
Suicidal behaviour : the search for psychic economy
1. Suicidal behaviour 2. Psychoanalysis
I. Title
616.8'582
ISBN 1 85302 788 X

Printed and Bound in Great Britain by
Athenaeum Press, Gateshead, Tyne and Wear

Contents

Contents

Introduction

What first led me to study suicide was fear and uncertainty. How are we to understand a suicidal development in a patient and assess the current risk of suicide? Then there is the fear that a patient may do away with himself. In some cases, suicidal patients tried to force me to make concessions, for instance a lady who said that unless I gave her permission for weekend leave she would kill herself. Given her scanty means of self-assertion, the threat had to be taken seriously. Anyone dealing with suicidal patients knows the feelings induced by such threats, the fear and anger, and in lengthy cases, the rage and helplessness. How is one to handle such feelings? What can one do other than try to suppress them? Only later did it become clear to me that such feelings and urges to act, although sometimes hard to bear, are rather valuable provided that the therapist can let them develop, for they can contain the key to the doctor–patient relation and thus lead to an understanding of the patient.

In the clinic, a colleague discussed with me a female patient of his who had killed herself some days previously. First he mentioned his feelings of guilt and then, after some hesitation, his impotent rage towards her, developed in the course of her therapy, so that in recent weeks he had more than once wished that she would go ahead and no longer torture him. He reported these feelings almost as a confessional. He went on to say that he did not know whom he should consult on their full import, from fear that a mistake might be imputed to him. After all, there was literature on the so-called 'induction of the bad, destructive object'. Why should this occur only from patient to therapist? Might the reverse not happen: the therapist transfers his destructive parts to the patient and thereby unwittingly contributes to the latter's self-destruction?

Such misgivings were familiar to me as well, though I had never made them explicit. When I raised the subject of countertransference feelings in the treatment of suicidal patients with colleagues, discussion usually became lively and serious. However, no general conclusion was drawn on how such insights could be used in therapy. One reason for this is that death by suicide implicitly lays blame on the therapist. More importantly, the therapist does so himself: witness the fact that when the circumstances are reconstructed, the emphasis is put on objective psychopathological data, while patient–nursing staff relations are deliberately neglected. Yet it is from countertransference data that we can make important inferences on the dynamics of suicide and on possible configurations of internal objects (which may have called for punishment or repentance).

The post-hoc diagnosis of a suicide often shifts the emphasis, for example by placing more weight on endogenous psychotic components than neurotic ones or borderline structure. Stressing an endogenous part in a patient who has killed himself permits a diagnosis divorced from relations. Such a somatogenetic diagnosis no longer aims at a fair assessment of the patient, but at describing the course of a disease without reference to the interaction between patient and therapist.

On the surface, this appears to favour the therapist, for it seems that the often intricate links built up between him and the patient during therapy have been suddenly resolved, so that he can feel exonerated. However, a residual unease remains, for he feels that he played a part in the formation of these links. In a sense he is right: his part was that of re-enacting a pathogenic object relation from early childhood.

Often therapists think that if they feel anger, hate, guilt or impotence when treating suicidal patients, they must have made a mistake and infer that in 'better' therapy such feelings could be avoided. This overlooks the fact that part of the therapist's task is to let such feelings arise and to endure them; this is his lot when treating any patient. With suicidal patients these feelings are usually guilt, impotent rage and hate based on dependence relations. The patient needs the therapist as someone who feels all this just as he does but can endure it and show him a way out. The therapist must therefore let these feelings, induced by the patient, arise within himself. He cannot erase them, and should not think that he ought not to have them because they poison the relation with the patient. The opposite is true: the relation becomes disinfected because the feelings express and follow on from interactions with important former and present reference persons, can be named and thereby captured and treated. This most fertile side of attempts at understanding suicidal developments is simply ignored if the attendant dynamics are severed from their part in the interaction and reduced to a one-dimensional event within the patient.

Post-hoc psychiatric accounts often hide the unacknowledged conviction that suicides of 'psychotherapy' patients as against 'psychiatric' ones should really be avoidable ('this sort of thing must not happen to me in my ward'). In my opinion this is a misunderstanding of guilt, as mentioned above: it views feelings of guilt not as a means of understanding a corresponding part of the patient but as a reaction to supposed failure. Moreover, it relieves one's own sense of failure by seeing suicide as psychopathological and thus distancing one from such behaviour.

Freud said that 'no neurotic intends suicide, unless he turns on himself a murderous impulse towards others' (Freud 1916, p.438). Federn, however, said that as a rule 'only he whom others wish dead kills himself' (1928/29, p.388). To wish another dead or to be wished dead by him seem at first opposing ideas, but as for suicide being an event between people, the two authors agree. In some cases it looks as if a patient wants to kill himself regardless of anyone else, without wishing to evoke guilt, repentance and the like, and without any clear 'appeal' (so well described by Stengel (1952, 1961)). Such cases call for great alarm, and for an attempt to return a process apparently severed from reference persons, to its real interpersonal form. This brings the therapist into play again. Although his task will be harder than before, his presence will allow the patient to relate to somebody again and so lessen the risk of suicide.

Freud's theory is based on the notion of object relations. Even if the ego aims at itself the aggression first aimed at the object, introjection ensures that the latter remains involved and intended in the process. It is hard to handle one's own aggressive streaks, but this is central in dealing with suicidal behaviour. Ringel (1969) speaks of 'pre-suicidal syndrome', a valuable means of recognising and assessing such behaviour. However, reducing Freud's theory to a purely internal aggressive conflict is a simplification (cf. Henseler 1984, p.62) in which object relations vanish. In the course of dealing with patients who had made repeated attempts at suicide and during whose therapy suicidal phases occurred, it seemed increasingly unavoidable to construe this not just as a sign of spiritual decay but also as a psychic function. It is a measure of last resort when inner or interpersonal crises seem no longer manageable. Thus I do not view suicidal behaviour as pathological, but as shorthand for complex rearrangements that point to a disordered handling of inner objects and self-images, our conscious and unconscious pictures of others. Suicidal behaviour is more than a sign of unintegrated aggressiveness: like any other symptom, it has a regulating function as well, and at times even a stabilising one, strange as this may sound.

Generic and specific suicidal behaviour

The risk of suicide is determined by two groups of factors. Generic factors include advanced age, loneliness, unemployment, life crises, psychiatric illness, and past abuse of drink, medicines or drugs, as well as the circumstances of earlier attempts at suicide. These factors determine the basic risk of suicide. A person subject to some of these need not yet be effectively suicidal. He becomes so only when triggering factors arise, such as the loss of an important reference person, serious and unbearable insult, or social exposure and the like. Such triggers can turn a generic form into an effective one. Here, object relations are vital, since general assessments of risk no longer suffice: the setting is a relation. Often it aims at a target person (the 'significant other'). In short, if generic suicidal behaviour turns into an actual crisis (which can take years), a further person, as a rule, enters the situation. This new relation, in which the patient shapes his specific form of suicidal behaviour, allows the other (in therapy, the therapist) to gain insight into the structure of the particular case. The study of the relation that the patient aspires to is thus a fertile means of assessing and treating effective suicidal behaviour.

Theoretical frame of reference

Any effective form of suicidal behaviour is closely linked with object experiences in early childhood, and is an expression of how these were internalised and how they structured the psyche. What has become self-evident for the psychic symptoms and specific patterns of object relations (cf., for example, collusion models (Willi 1975)) holds for formations of suicidal object relations as well. Balint is right in pointing out 'that even in the deepest psychic layers barely accessible to analysis, object relations predominate'; it is they that 'in principle determine the weal and woe of the individual' (cited by Hoffmeister 1977, p.121). This means that behind manifest behaviour we must consistently look for conflictive object relations. Hence to grasp and decode the psychodynamics and function of suicide we must note the developmental stage at which the situation leading to such behaviour occurs. Henseler (Henseler and Reimer 1981, p.156) points out that 'conscious conflict leading to a suicidal crisis … is as a rule merely an occasion when a long existing though unconscious conflict is inflamed anew.' The psychoanalytic theory of object relations thus provides the most flexible framework for understanding suicidal behaviour. In this book I shall discuss those stages from early childhood that offer important guidelines.

In the transition from pre-psychotic to borderline levels and thence to integrative ones, the attendant steps in development expose the psyche to special demands and stresses. We usually meet a particular patient not at a particular level, but in a field of transitional tensions in which he is trying to move ahead and develop; this may make him afraid of what to him is new and unaccustomed, and could at times lead him back to more familiar territory.

In both transitional domains, suicidal behaviour may occur, but with different meanings and goals.

First transitional domain

The region between pre-psychotic and borderline function can be linked to images in which suicidal behaviour corresponds to regulative functions in the to and fro of building and removing limits between self and objects. The infant must learn to distinguish what is part of him and what is not. Later, he must be able to bear that this non-self, if human, consists of independent individuals who think, plan and do things that are nothing to do with him. This developmental step usually creates a fear of being abandoned. A return to the familiar earlier state reduces this fear. In this domain we are thus faced with forms of suicidal behaviour that obey the principle of return to the familiar undivided, described by terms like fusion, reunion, search for the lost symbiosis. Authors such as Henseler (1975), Meissner (1977) and Richman (1978), to name but a few, have studied this. The dynamics of such behaviour has been well explored and is generally known. This is where the thesis of the wish to merge with the 'primary object' is held. What, however, would it mean if psychic fusion actually occurred? One of its motives is the hope for boundless shelter, since one would have fused with the sheltering object. This wish naturally provokes fear, since it wants to seduce the ego to shed its autonomy and boundaries: the ego reacts with this warning signal. The fear of fusion is a vital ally in maintaining the ego's autonomy, its boundaries or its attained psychic growth, or whatever we wish to call it. The wish to merge is usually taken to express regressive forces, which aim at restoring earlier stages of development in an interpersonal setting where such regressive dependence ('being a part of someone') can flourish. Conversely, the fear of fusion therefore expresses antiregressive forces. Every person has both poles of this field of tension; indeed he must possess them, if he is to be able adequately to enjoy and relax as well as to work, plan and decide.

What if the accustomed guidelines (which usually remain unconscious and need not be consciously acknowledged) no longer suffice to counter regressive forces, so that the fear of fusion must invoke its warning role? Here, suicidal behaviour, which earlier promised to fulfil the desire to merge' may be activated – not now in the fantasy of entering and being welcome in a boundless shelter, but in rallying the ego to do something that nobody else can influence further, for which I alone am responsible to myself, independent and bounded. The person feels severed from others and becomes suicidal. The wish to merge thus triggers the fear that it may be realised: it seems that this fact has so far hardly been discussed as a possible source of suicide. There is much literature on 'fear of being swallowed up by the primary object' (cf., for example, Abelin 1975; Rotmann 1978; Zagerman 1988); but the question whether the opposite case, of suicidal behaviour as reaction against fusion, can play a role has hardly been touched either in theory or in clinical practice. Here, the psychoanalytic theory of object relations might guide research into suicidal behaviour, and suggests vital prospects especially in clinical therapy.

Thus one may misconstrue the suicidal behaviour of a seemingly less helpless patient and imagine that he needs special protection from everyday worries and burdens, since he is supposed to be unable to bear further problems. This may indeed be so in some cases, although such cases seem rather rare. However, under therapeutic treatment such a patient may more and more often develop suicidal thoughts and tendencies. In clinical cases, one usually not only offers a patient who turns suicidal more sessions but also treats him more cautiously. This may further intensify his suicidal tendency: a vicious circle, based on misconstruing his message of suicidal behaviour. In such cases the concept of anti-fusing function of suicidal tendencies may be of help, for it may suggest that the symptom now resists an offer that leads to an uncomfortable closeness. It would be an offer that bypassed the ego's endeavour to be autonomous and directly addressed and reinforced the patient's regressive tendencies. The patient's reaction to the institutional offer of regression may be to consider methods of suicide: the patient defends himself to protect his endangered ego. Paradoxically, what was meant to help may threaten. Just so, the path to the motorway bridge, and a glance at cars that may kill, no longer express regressive merging tendencies, but rather make the ego more coherent: here I am, alone responsible for myself.

Second transitional domain

In the transition from borderline function to integration, the links are different. Here it is no longer a matter of maintaining ego boundaries with the primary object. Now that ego and non-ego have been fairly well severed, there are objects that one may confront. How will they react? Since we can no longer hold fusion fantasies, is there not a danger that the objects may abandon us? Since we have become stronger as persons, should we not turn away from them if they disappoint? In that case, are we not then alone again? This domain is about dealing with objects that in their new and autonomous form are as yet unfamiliar. We strive to keep objects lasting and reliable, and are uncertain whether we can feel them to be so. Experience soon shows that they are not, for objects are capricious and inconstant: an object that at first sight seems promising and trustworthy can quickly disappoint. This is the domain of 'good' and 'bad' objects as devised by Melanie Klein (1946). Besides, what of oneself? Another may now view us as important and interesting, but then suddenly lose interest and form other plans, from which one infers that one has become boring to him, or indeed to everybody.

The second transitional domain is also the phase in which the structures that regulate self-esteem are set up. This can arise only if one is sure that others have a good image of oneself, figuring oneself as a good object. Only then can one internalise an image of self-esteem, without which one cannot live.

This transitional domain is a time of moving object relations and therefore of turbulent phases of therapy as well, where not everything that is fought out in the interpersonal field can be viewed as 'acting' in the classical sense. The patient is not yet in sufficient command of psychic structures to enable him to absorb the interaction into the intrapsychic area. He is less concerned with avoiding becoming conscious than with the developing and maturing of psychic structures. The basic uncertainty in relations between people, the rapid change of partners, the rapid alterations in experiencing self-esteem, all these are linked with as yet poorly integrated images of self and objects at this level. It is the time of Dr Jekyll and Mr Hyde. It is impressive to experience the battles of patients who are trying to bring opposing images of self and objects closer together, while increasing that distance in case of failure. How tenaciously they accept inevitable attendant disappointments; and how they must retreat and start, full of hate for self and others, to reorganise the disappointed self; and how the wish to live in an earlier more familiar but more limited world, with objects that are only good or only bad, alternates with the striving towards new relations that allow a greater range of autonomy.

A difficulty in approaching a 'depressive position' (Klein 1946) is that we must recognise that every disappointment, and also every attention, protection and promotion, that we have experienced stems from one and the same person. We always regarded him as mean, cold, heartless, and as one who betrayed us (because he turned to others too), and we therefore wished he was dead, yet at the same time we respected and loved him. That this arouses strong inner tumult in which the patient has to exert his whole power to steer his way through is not surprising. In these integrating processes that aim at a depressive position we may expect a new form of suicidal behaviour, linked to the feelings of guilt and despair typical for this phase of development and therapy.

The reflections presented in this book do not claim to be applicable to all forms of suicidal behaviour. The goal is more narrow and follows from observations in clinical psychoanalytic and psychotherapeutic cases of neurotics, psychosomatic patients and borderline disorders. Not included are for instance patients who suffer from incurable organic diseases and manifest psychotics. For countertransference it is one thing if a paranoid hallucinatory psychotic attempts suicide by following commanding voices, another if after pharmaceutical treatment of depressive stupor a patient's ego is suddenly overrun by delusions of guilt and he reacts by suicide, and another still if a neurotic or borderline case tries by suicidal behaviour to create a certain object relation. This last form is aimed rather more clearly at a target person; the previous form for the psychotic does this too, but can more easily be severed from the doctor–patient relation. In sum, my basic assumptions are these:

1. Suicidal behaviour is subject to regulatory processes, within and between persons. To view it as a psychic lack of compensation is inadequate. Like other psychic symptoms, it expresses a psychic effort in a state of crisis that at the time cannot be mastered otherwise.

2. Such behaviour arises where there are conflictive relations to inner objects and aspects of self, set in early phases of development.

3. Such behaviour resides within a relation, even if this relation no longer exists (e.g. vengeance on a father with whom one has been out of touch for years, by imagining that one might move him to repentance).

4. The degree of understanding of such behaviour in a given patient depends on how far we manage to find and grasp the pathogenic object experience of early childhood.

5. If the main features of these object experiences become manifest in transference and countertransference, we can identify suicidal dynamics from the doctor–patient relation. The analysis of countertransference is vital here.

6. Suicidal behaviour primarily expresses the wish to change an object relation, not the desire to die. However, the need for death may follow from a failure to change the object relation.

7. Even an actual suicide need not primarily have expressed a wish to die, but may have taken action in a final attempt to change the object ('I will kill myself so that you will regret what you have done to me, and thus become an object well disposed towards me'). Suicide thus remains an interactional means and not an end in itself.

8. The term 'self-murder' no longer fits this mode of approach. Suicidal behaviour is more like taking the ego as hostage from the self, with the aim to change an object and a relation. Just as the hostage-taker does not mean to kill his victim but wants to use the hostage to compel an external object to behave in a certain way, so the suicidal patient uses the threat to his self to change an external object and his relation to it.

9. The point is to find an object that will make one's existence feel justified; without it one cannot live.

1

The Dynamics of Keeping Apart and Merging in the First Transitional Domain
(Pre-psychotic to Borderline Levels)

Three landmarks on the way to integration

The psychoanalytic theory of object relations describes stages of early childhood development:

1. Developing the categories of 'good' and 'evil' as a precondition for roughly distinguishing between pleasant and unpleasant experiences.

2. Keeping apart what belongs to oneself from what belongs to the external world (formation of the categories of 'self' and 'not-self').

3. Abolishing a world view split into wholly good and wholly bad (integration of good and bad representations of self and objects).

As regards distinguishing the various events and experiences flooding in on the infant into positive and negative, Kernberg (1981) speaks of 'valencies'. The idea is that all experiences of the same valency merge into a total picture, so that we end up with one positive and one negative image of ourselves and of objects. If this state persists into adulthood, we risk overrating and idealising, or devaluing, ourselves and our

was as if she abruptly covered a camera lens, took on a set attitude
and hid behind a mask. If she had come too close before, now she
seemed too distant.

On the one hand a person desires the other's permanent presence; on
the other they may abruptly drop the object if it announces wishes of its
own or the relation becomes more demanding. Dealing with, for example, a games machine can be seen to illustrate such a situation: by using
the 'risk' button one can become further and further removed from the
zero line, until the score collapses (in most cases), the gambler loses
everything and falls back to solid ground (zero level). In this way a
patient can externalise his inner dilemma. He asks for an optimal
distance from the object for safety and comfort, and time and again he
finds there is none; either he is too close or too distant and movements
away or back are attempts at regulating interpersonal distance (Kind
1988).

Since being too close and too distant are equally dangerous, these
extreme movements are a highly significant system of regulation. Just as
a comet moves between minimal and maximal distance from the central
star and neither falls into it nor breaks away from it, so the patient not
yet sufficiently freed from symbiosis tries to avoid both dangers:

- Excessive approach to the object risks symbiotic fusion,
  destroying the boundaries of self and identity. (We shall shortly
  see at this pole of regression a certain fear which forces the
  subject to return, thus avoiding further regression.)

- Excessive distance risks destroying relation with the object.
  Here it is useful to have a fear that forces the subject to return.

In the myth of Icarus the dynamics of this regulating system is well captured: when he and his father escaped from a Cretan prison using wings
that Daedalus had made from feathers and wax, the young man ignored
his father's warning not to fly too near the sun. The wax melted and
south of Samos he fell into the sea since then called after him.

Icarus moves between the poles of labyrinth and flying high. He cannot stay at either and is forced to retreat from each. In the labyrinth it is the monster Minotaur, in flight the sun that prevents further approach. Icarus' dilemma is his failure to achieve the middle height that Daedalus had recommended.

This dilemma is typical of many psychic phenomena connected with detachment from the symbiotic object. We may compare it to the phase of detachment and individuation alternating with renewed approach (Mahler 1979).

Labyrinth and flying high, Minotaur and Icarus, can be seen as poles of a system that goes into action when the psychic structures are not yet able to reach an optimal distance from the object (middle height of flight, ego-determined use of the risk button on the games machine). The two poles balance each other.

In a dream a patient turned the two poles between which he tried to organise his object relations into a flexible image:

> I am in a swimming bath. Gravity is annulled and I can walk on the water. Then I ascend some stairs but am afraid of the door at the top. I reach winding and complex corridors with branches but do not know which to take. Something invisible surrounds me and comes ever nearer. At last I am back at the door, look back but cannot see anybody. I can walk only slowly now as if a little lame. On closing the door behind me, the fear vanishes, as does the feeling of being pursued. I am back in the bath but under normal gravity. I have to descend the stairs quite normally.

The narcissist fantasy of being able to walk on water is replaced by a regression leading to a labyrinth, arrested in turn by the fear of a pursuer.

This patient had a delicate feeling for such 'icaroid' boundary situations where he was on the threshold of detachment from the object and renewed approach. He reported the following:

> I took a bend in my car at 120 km/h. The road surface was somewhat slippery. I wondered if the car would take it. It did.

> When I go surfing I move far out so that the beach becomes a narrow strip and the people look like small points. Around me complete silence. I am quite alone. Splendid.

In Icarus situations one aims for the narrow zone of balance between centrifugal and centripetal forces. There the tendency to detach from the object is arrested by the fear of object loss, so that wish and fear are in balance. The resulting tension produces the thrill that Balint (1960) has examined in detail. The surfer moves out to a limit where visual contact with people still exists, a bend in the road is taken at a speed within a certain limit for the balance of centripetal force and friction to be maintained. One enters situations that fascinate because of the risk of breaking away from the primary object Mother Earth. At the same time one creates conditions that protect against irreversible change.

So, too, for the scientists in Jules Verne's *Journey to the Centre of the Earth*: Professor Lidenbrock and his nephew run into a labyrinth of passages far below ground. There they meet their own phylogenetic unconscious in the form of prehistoric animal and human creatures. It is a trip into the depths of the past. Return is forced by a huge flood that washes them back to the surface.

In all these examples we have variations on the mechanism of the counterregressive principle. This regressive pole of the regulating system is of special interest for fusionary and anti-fusionary forms of suicidal behaviour, of which more later. The fantasy leading to distancing (flying, hovering, walking on water) is interrupted by a regressive movement. To prevent this from assuming a dimension beyond what is therapeutically usable (malign regression) a deterrent being protects us. Its position is the state of deep regression, symbolised by the principle of the labyrinth, where it is the guardian opposing malign regression.

The labyrinth as metaphor for the unknown interior of surrounding objects and of ourselves makes us curious and incites us to invade its territory. One explores the object or oneself. One penetrates, as Lidenbrock does in Jules Verne's tale, or one enters one's own interior in the sense of 'regression in the service of the ego' (for example in analysis). This produces fear of not being able to find the way back. One can lay a trail of breadcrumbs but still get lost in the forest like Hansel and Gretel and meet one's own unconscious in various forms, for example a witch. With Jules Verne it is the fear of having to stay at the centre of the Earth. In analytic psychotherapy it is the fear of malign regression.

Individuation in the myth of creation: another perspective of early triangulation

In the literature on suicidal psychodynamics there are many references (sometimes a little one-sided) to the hypothesis of fusion, the thesis of connection with the primary object. This object is then 'the maternal principle', 'the archaic mother', 'the Great Mother' (Neumann 1987), to mention but a few names. The thesis of the devouring symbiotic maternal object from which the undertow to regression starts, plays a great role in the concepts of 'early' (as regards development) forms of suicidal behaviour.

However, we must not allow accepted concepts to constrict our views too much. It makes a good deal of therapeutic difference whether for emerging suicidal behaviour one goes by a regressive concept that starts from a female principle of undertow, or whether one looks for the patient's regressive desires. The two need not exclude each other, and intervention will be guided by what the patient offers; but it is inevitable that one will pursue goals in terms of concepts that one has adopted.

One may therefore ask why the regressive tendency that everyone has and needs is projected onto the archaic mother. A provisional answer might be that female sexual anatomy lends itself better to represent the goal of regression, since the tendency not only points back in time (i.e. to an earlier phase in the development of libido), but also inwards. Why, though, does this tendency common to both genders become an undertow towards just one? Is the female gender marked by a feature that does not belong to it as such? If so, from where was the

The creation myth explains that part of the goal of the regressive tendency which can no longer be identified with a 'mistaken feminine'. The desire for regression is not aimed at the woman, who exerts a regressive undertow, but it is God who has forbidden crossing the boundary from primary process to the ego-ruled secondary one, and it is Adam who wants to stay with the regressive object (God), while Eve begins to detach him from it by seducing him to thought.

If the triangulating function can take up only an object that differs enough in quality from the primary object, it follows that in paradise this function must be feminine. If God thought that 'it is not good that the man should be alone; I will make him an help meet for him' (Genesis 2:18), it was surely sensible, anticipating the triangulation needed later, to create a woman, an object sufficiently different to be able to take on this role. Separation gives scope for further development, but it also involves risk, for one can get lost in a space that without other symbiotic objects must be imagined empty. However, it cannot be avoided: without it, there is no individuation, or becoming a subject.

Often we meet forms of regression that imply a threat to the boundary between self and not-self. The forces needed to maintain this vital boundary fall off, or other opposite ones, seeking to remove it, begin to dominate. We speak of an insecure or permeable self-object boundary. Clinically this shows itself by increased occurrence of projective and introjective mechanisms; i.e. the subject will attribute more of his own features to others and take on certain features of others for himself, thus eroding what marks him from others.

If one is able to tell good from bad, integrated experience of them is a mixed bundle of qualities of all people including oneself. But the experience still presents difficulties: preferred relations are formed in which one person becomes bearer of everything bad, and another of everything good, including the good features projected by the subject.

This projective transformation of self-image and object-image can be strengthened by introjective processes running parallel to it: they cause alien aspects of good and bad to be taken into one's own self. Two goals may be aimed at here:

- either the subject can feel close to, and wish to be linked with, a mainly good object (or one made so by projection, projective identification and the like);

- or the subject can feel mainly bad and evil, and pursued by an object he made so (through the same mechanisms).

If the mainly positive case prevails, the subject will tend to merge with the object, since it is pleasant to know oneself linked with such an object. A deep connection with the object will be sought and a deep entry made into it. There it will, however, come to fear losing its ego-boundaries and therefore summon up the negative object-image which now demands the distance of a pursuer.

Returning to suicidal behaviour, it will be clear that it can take on roles in both domains. It can express the subject's wish to merge with the object, but also serve to set limits when the subject feels the danger of losing its ego. It can further the wish for merging (fusing suicidal behaviour) or serve the forces that sense merging only as a danger and want to deflect it (anti-fusing).

2

Suicidal Behaviour between Pre-psychotic and Borderline Levels
(First Transitional Domain)

Fusing suicidal behaviour (connection in the beyond)

After his girl friend had left him, a patient felt agitated and driven for a while. Then he developed a suicide fantasy and plan. He bought tablets and took a car into an area he knew from a joint holiday with her. There he bought wine and sought out a corner he knew well, to kill himself at dusk.

Another lady patient had written a farewell letter and had settled various important matters before travelling to the seaside to look for a site where she might kill herself. She absorbed the rushing of the waves and became calm at the idea of being carried out to sea to be dissolved in it.

A third patient had for some years entertained the fantasy that he had to kill himself in the same way as his aunt had done. He thought of death as release and believed in an afterlife. He reported that his aunt, who had brought him up in lieu of a son, had killed herself when he was still a child. He had often seen her attempts and tried to make her refrain, and had alerted doctors and hospitals. He imagined he would be with her after his death, but was afraid of going ahead.

We have seen that in the course of the first step of differentiation, in which the child eats, and must eat, from the tree of knowledge, two great psychic structures arise, symbolised by one figure that embodies sort of suicidal behaviour give their papers titles like 'Reunion with the mother' (Meissner 1977), 'Restoration of a lost symbiosis' (Richman 1978), 'Fusing with a diffusely experienced early object' (Henseler 1975), 'Return into the maternal body' (Fischer 1986). We must examine whether the patient in whom this tendency prevails still has opposite, anti-fusing forces at his command.

Above, we briefly mentioned a patient ruled by a fantasy that he must die as his aunt had. He was referred for therapy from a psychiatric clinic because of recurrent flare-ups of suicidal behaviour. He had suffered from these for years and had made several attempts at killing himself. Since his aunt's death he had been pursued by the notion of having to end his life. Without visible inner involvement he reported this and was intent on appearing unconcerned while the case history was taken. The ward doctor reported that she soon took an interest in him, but felt as if captured by him and unable to tear herself away. This countertransferential feeling was an important finding that gave her essential psychodynamic hints. The patient wanted to understand his fusing fantasy through therapy so that he might distance himself from it, in turn making someone else feel a prisoner. The interactional means was his way of dealing with the antisuicide pact. A genuine pact could not be concluded with him: 'Either one does away with oneself, or not; but one does not talk about it,' he told his therapist. This tempted her constantly to worry about him. She was never quite sure whether he would or not, and if so, when. She seemed to be in the same position with him as he had been with his aunt, who by her many attempts had shown that she might kill herself any time, and for whom he had felt responsible. His role then he had handed on to his therapist, who now felt responsible for him while he in his suicidal ways identified with his aunt. Suicide was always possible, it was in the air. His relation with the therapist had developed aspects that had previously marked his relation with the aunt. This repetition enabled the therapist to step out of the current relation with the patient and to tell him that he was now behaving towards her as his aunt had done towards him and that she would not let him. She told him that he was responsible for his own life and not she, just as his aunt had been for hers and not he.

In such situations one must be clear that therapy does not cease because the patient wants to repeat a pathogenic pattern or break an antisuicide pact, but that on the contrary it moves to a decisive point where the patient offers his therapist a deep insight into a central conflictual relation. Since the therapist now felt as he had done, namely that she was now the carrier of the unbearable state of constant worry about someone whose suicide was an ever-present possibility, he had enabled her to understand an essential feature of his fear. This amazing process of projective identification has often been described; more about this later. In his room, this patient had put up a poster on which a serpent grows out of the muscular upper arm of a man, bending towards the arm and about to bite it. Why this poster? Was this to give someone a hint of something that he felt in himself? Did he perhaps feel threatened by an inner object, and this was his way to describe the threat, naming it and so getting a hold on it?

After an intense friendship with a woman, of whom he reported that she had shared his bed for a year, the patient had had many brief affairs. When he felt hemmed in, which mostly meant that a woman wanted something more definite from him, he cooled off and the relation soon ended. In the ward, this charming young man had soon become popular with many women. He sat amongst them and there was mutual liking. Harmony reigned, no disturbance. However, he felt empty, and excluded. 'Nobody really knows me, or what makes me run.'

I did not ask him how he really ran, but enquired about his fear of being known or recognised by another, with the question: 'Do you really want to be known?'

Patient: In one way yes, why not, that would be nice.

I: And in another?

P.: I do not know, somehow it is eerie. You must be genuine then, and listen to the other. I do not know whether I want this, whether I

This removes splitting from the group of primitive defence mechanisms in as far as we must postulate a synthetic ego-function that sums these collaborating mechanisms into the clinical phenomenon.

If we can resolve splitting into its constituents, we must be able to do the same with integration too. This thus becomes the result of combined partial processes: for example, the result of taking back-projection, projective identification, of retracting pathological idealisation and giving up devaluation, leading to a greater capacity to perceive realistically. It is not simply the case that growing integration makes projection superfluous, and unmasks idealisation and devaluation as mistakes while it frees our vision for reality and occupies areas hitherto denied; rather the other way round: only steady and constant individual action of all these mechanisms finally leads to what we call integration of good and bad aspects of self and objects.

If we allow that splitting involves the ego in a complex and psychically heavy operation, we must suppose that the resulting psychic products matter to it. What is created is split 'good' and 'bad' images of self and objects.

Projection of the negative split image

This is often observed; it is used to counter a threat to stable boundaries between self and objects. At times one gains the impression that negative object images are a sort of protective shield raised against the real outer object, to avoid too close a contact with it. As an unconscious process this will not be perceived by the subject, but experienced as a deterrent quality of the object. Here is an example:

> One night at the clinic, the duty doctor called me because a patient seemed to be acting strangely. He no longer understood her and was afraid that she might become psychotic. She said that she had tried to absorb the negative side of her fellow patients and to neutralise this by her own counter forces. However, she had only partly succeeded in this. She could still feel the negative effects of the others in herself. That is why she had fallen into deep prayer to

God that afternoon, to take on his strength. In the end she had felt God very close to her and totally carrying her. At that moment she had been afraid that she might not come out of this state. She had gone to speak to the doctor on duty in the ward. He had not understood her problems so that she had argued with him and accused him of not trying to understand her inner cares. They quarrelled. Unfortunately the state she had been in when praying was gone. The fault was the insensitive duty doctor's (evidently a good therapist, since he offered a face-to-face meeting in which she could test how far she agreed with him and where she differed from him).

In coming intensely close to an omniscient and omnipotent purely good object, the patient's ego sent a signal of fear, pointing to the danger of fusion. The duty doctor, whom she regarded as careless, had in fact seen an important function in this near-psychotic regression: he did not understand everything, and so was not an object with which one could merge. This quality (in the patient's conscious experience a defect) allowed her to project on him a negative object image, which showed itself in the debate with him. This distancing revived a feeling for the boundary between self and object; it could not occur with the omniscient and therefore dangerous object and had provoked fear as a warning signal.

Here we are close to the boundary between borderline and psychotic regression. The concept of borderline regression covers a wide range: some such structures are very stable and adopt marked defences that lead to splitting only under stress, without sliding into near-psychotic experiences. Then there are patients, like the one just described, who under stress are easily threatened by the loss of boundaries between self and object and as a last defence against near-merging regression use suicidal behaviour. Let me first clarify the dynamics in the area of unstable boundaries between self and object by means of another example:

> In an admission interview an 'open' atmosphere soon developed, and the patient told me a lot about herself. She spoke of her suicide

attempts and suicide dreams, in which she jumped from great heights and hit the ground. In relations she always made 'belly landings' but did not know why. When she took leave, I felt I had learnt more about her than is usual at a first meeting. Had she jumped into a relation with me as in her dreams. If so, how had she landed? At the end I had told her that next time she was to go on about what she felt to be most important to her, if she wanted to.

At the next session her behaviour changed. She was suspicious and felt that she was being questioned and squeezed dry and persecuted by me. The turning point was my question about her last suicide attempt. We had briefly touched on it at the first meeting, but now she no longer wanted to talk about it. Suddenly I become an envious, persecuting person. My questions were false, I chose the wrong words and stressed them in a disdainful way. I had a rejecting and overbearing streak, denying her qualities.

How is this change to be taken? I think that the first time she felt tempted to link herself closely to a good object that tried to understand her; a feeling so strong that she had to find a way to feel distant enough to resume autonomy. As the one who sought understanding and therefore connection, I had become dangerous (hence the fear of fusion), so that she had to project on me the rejecting aspect of the object and look for negative qualities in me. When she had succeeded in this, the preconditions were present for having to seek distance from me, and for being able to do so. Her ego had recognised the danger of a tendency to merge and had produced a timely transformation of the person concerned into a bad and persecuting object that must be watched. That is how she achieved timely reserve. But once again she made a belly landing. I, too, did not understand her. Indeed, I had not adequately recognised the danger to her of being understood. This must have been painful to her conscious experience, but the price for the self was small compared with the gain of having avoided a fusion-based malign ego-regression.

Strange as it may sound, to attend to and understand another is not free of danger for oneself, at any rate not when it concerns areas that can be taken on by the therapist. In patients with pre-psychotic structure, understanding comes to be the same as agreeing, being of the same opinion and having no differences. Such a dynamics of levelling between subject and object easily enters the zone where two persons turn into one, which means psychic death for one of them. The attempt to understand the other can then destabilise the boundary between I and thou. In the effort to understand the patient one must therefore always keep an eye on how far he can bear nearness and agreement. One must empathise with his insecurity about protection of this boundary. This further means that one must allow that the other, like everybody, needs areas of non-agreement. Only if we grasp that a patient may fear to be understood can we do justice to him. This is not always made easy. If one disagrees with the patient, he does not usually experience this as expressing different points of view, rather he feels misunderstood and rejected. A therapist might then think that he must locate this 'misunderstanding', in order to clear it, since he wants to understand the patient rather than misunderstand him. The therapist's intensified attempt to understand then often leads to a vicious circle: the patient becomes afraid of being too near, defends himself against the therapist's offer by saying that he feels misunderstood, so that he can establish sharper boundaries again and stabilise his ego. The therapist, using a mistaken concept of 'understanding', tries to remove this 'misunderstanding' (needed by the patient for stability), and thereby unwittingly attacks an anti-regressive wall of disagreement precariously propped up by the patient. Sometimes it helps to say: 'We seem to disagree here', or 'I have not understood you here.'

The negative object image seems to become active at the critical moment when the psyche, in the course of regression, fears having its ego-boundaries destabilised (cf. Zagermann 1988). Such situations are often observed, if one looks out for them. Regression is triggered by, for example, disappointments that provoke anger. To protect oneself and the object from this anger, one can seek connection with an omnipotent entirely good object. This is a critical point: destabilisation of ego-boundaries. If now the negative object-image becomes active and is projected on the other, the main danger is usually past, though clinically one often notices only now what the matter is (or rather was). When this projection onto a real person has occurred, the process becomes interpersonal again and it becomes easier once more to insert oneself. In his own view, the patient experiences this new rejecting and distancing attitude as the right reaction to the object perceived as disappointing, which may of course be a quite realistic perception and assessment. However, this attitude might also serve as a defence against fusion (that is the aspect we are concerned with here). In that case one has the impression that the patient simply must find something negative in his therapist, thus justifying distance.

This frequent but always amazing process is possible only with the help of splitting, which provides for the ego the necessary negative image.

Scapegoats and witches: recipients of the negative split image

In the examples above, negative images of self and objects were projected onto real persons. Sometimes there are no such targets; instead we meet deterrent figures of fantasy: witches, dark ladies, demons.

It seems hard to live without witches, without the incarnation of what one takes to be bad. The fantasy figure of the witch as bearer of one's own instinctual impulses evidently can stabilise both individuals and larger social structures and institutions. The Inquisition has testified to this, and the phenomenon does not belong only to the past. The idea that a real outer object enables us to express and discard inner stress is ancient and is based on the mechanism of projection ('throwing forward'), which must have come early in the history of evolution. The Old Testament states it correctly in the myth of the scapegoat: a primarily innocent object is burdened by the sinner with his own disapproved deeds and chased out into the desert far enough to prevent a return. The Greeks had a different mechanism: bad dreams were for them real entities that visited the sleeper at night. If no priest was available, one could talk a bad dream into a lump of clay. The clay now carried the badness and could be dissolved in a river and swept away (cf. Bergmann 1966). Objects like scapegoats and clay as bearers (or containers, as Bion put it) for alien psychic material are steps in the evolution of psychic structures.

We need witches, scapegoats and images of enemies to relieve stress. When we burn them or chase them into the desert, we need no longer struggle with what is bad in ourselves.

Beyond relieving stress, these objects that we have created have a further task: to produce distance. One keeps at a distance an object that has been transformed into a deterrent witch or the like. To initiate such a transformation, two conditions must be fulfilled:

- the object must be seductive (otherwise it would not be dangerous); and
- the subject must have an underdeveloped ego that cannot control its nearness to such attractive objects and reacts with fear.

These two preconditions (a wish urging on and a fear of braking) are in a conflict that must be resolved. If the subject lacks the strength to face such an object undiluted, he can still turn it into the opposite: one object (attractive) is replaced by another (repellent).

So long as the boundaries between subject and object are not stable enough, the splitting mechanism must be quickly recallable, to prepare the antithetical images of self and objects which can then stabilise the ego-boundaries against fusion. For the borderline level we can say that stabilisation of ego-boundaries occurs under the protection of splitting. The negative object-image must be seen in the other and therefore be projected on him whenever defectively protected ego-boundaries would mean merging with the object when it comes too near.

comes possible to give things a name or symbolise them, e.g. when the hitherto undreamable becomes dreamable, this not only starts further psychotherapeutic work but is already a result of earlier structuring.)

> A patient, who in her previous dreams was mainly alone in cold and steep areas, put the formation of self-objects into a dream in which she travelled on a timber cart connected by a long rod to a tractor. The driver had all the means to travel across the uneven ground. She had to grab the side so as not to fall out (which she did not). She was amazed that the driver could steer and brake without accident.

The rough trip corresponded to the previous months of her analysis, which moved over rough ground too. She still needed a self-object that could drive, control speed, accelerate and brake. Here analysis still had much to do. However, she had made marked progress in her analysis. Till now she was in danger of sliding off steep slopes and falling from skyscrapers, without being able to steer, brake or hold on to something. Only waking up forestalled worse, namely hitting the ground and possible break-up of the ego. This had not so far happened, as she had always been able to go into secondary process and wake up. In her real relation to me this meant the ability to call me in time when a psychic fall was threatening. (When a patient can no longer do this, the therapist must step in unasked.) Now, however, something else was afoot: the dream points to the patient daring to take up a relation with the therapist, and this relation need not break even in rough territory (disappointments in the analysis were tolerable and digestible). This shows much progress from the falling dreams of the previous phase of therapy.

It is not always the case that a patient has adequate psychic means to shape his dream so as to wake in time to avoid a fall:

> A patient of about 40 years of age, who had experienced many years of varied drug abuse, chronic suicidal behaviour and several attempts to kill herself, recalled in her initial clinical dream a concrete playground in which she is standing on top of the unprotected platform on a high tower. A storm sweeps her down

and she feels the impact and everything in her breaks. People say: 'We shall not be able to put her together again.'

('Initial clinical dream' is my term for a dream on admission, where we can assume that the fact of being admitted was part of the trigger and thus was probably worked into the dream.)

This is the dream, rare in my view, of the self-fragmenting. Nothing in the dreamer would rely on help in restoring her self. For some time we were worried by her, for we could not be sure that in a 'fall' caused by an insult or a loss of object she would be able to catch herself; on the contrary, by her initial dream she had told us that there was as yet no such safety net. At the same time we could be glad that by this dream she had informed us how unsure she felt in spite of her smile and radiated confidence. Some months later she reported a dream in which she was in a pool on a ship with bows of glass. People in the pool need her help but she refuses her hand for fear of being smashed herself.

In this connection she remembers her husband, a man who she fears will drown if she does not give him her hand. At the same time she begins to suspect that she will be shattered if some more room for movement is not imported into this relation. The clinic as self-object does indeed carry her, but she knows how fragile the whole thing is, like glass, and that she is not yet strong enough to be able to assist others who also need help. Compared with the first dream, the later dream shows that her unconscious is beginning to foresee what leads to a fall; e.g. in relations she must try to see herself as not fragmented if she is to help others by her own abilities unless she accounts for this to herself. We assessed this dream as a sign of progress, and it may have been. However, in our optimism we forgot how long psychic restructuring takes. When the patient was discharged she was not yet stable enough to protect her ego in stressful situations. Some weeks later we heard that she had killed herself.

In clinical psychotherapy one works against time. Costs will be borne only for a limited period. Besides, it is not advisable to treat a patient in a hospital for too long, because he loses too many social skills or angered her; e.g. bad marks, or friends of his she disliked. His mother valued that he did not contradict her nor put up views of his own, but she deplored his lack of professional progress and that he still depended on her financially.

In the ward, the patient liked dusk, dressed in black, and sat in the living room with other young men playing loud music. He sought settings where contours vanished and the other becomes no longer recognisable and distinguishable from oneself. In his room there were posters on which armed men kicked down skyscrapers with their hard military boots and destroyed cities with their bare fists. In therapeutic conversation his attitude was at first obedient, always agreeing; but one felt that no true rapport had been created.

An image of his father came only from the mother's stories. Her image of her husband which she drew in talks with her son became his father-image, from which he learnt that he had a bad father. That he could not accept. In this context we must mention a dream in which he sees himself in his grandmother's bedroom.

> The patient is fetched by huge men in black robes (he was a theology student) and taken to the cellar. There he is to free people behind grates, but fails to do so. He is taken back to the bedroom and notes that the floor is soft and has holes into which one can sink.

It was hoped that the intervention of the men in black would be successful and that he would not have to return to the domain of the mother, which was soft but held the risk of sinking. However, his dream was regressive, which occurred to me when some months after his discharge I learnt that he had committed suicide, probably after his lady friend had left him. Evidently we therapists had been unable to make him choose another way, as he had hoped that we might, even if we wore no robes or coats. When we discharged him he evidently had not yet found a way other than return to symbiotic objects, of which he had said that he could sever himself from them only by suicide.

This patient was trying in many ways to eliminate anything that separated him from others. At the same time he created barriers by destruction: of his skin, of cities in fantasy and then of himself by suicide.

Let us pursue a hint that this patient gave in his case history and in repeated dreams, and the significance of the father for the development of those psychic structures that make self-object boundaries possible.

For a symbiotic pair, separation into self and not-self is not possible. To initiate this process and carry it through successfully a third 'triangulating' person must appear, offering the precondition for the child to take up a qualitatively different relation from that with the primary object. If this precondition is satisfied, the symbiotic relation can gradually be opened up. Eve was distant enough from the primary object God, because she could distinguish herself adequately, thus initiating the prising loose of Adam. Such an object enables the child individuating itself to form a further connection and turn to this further object. Since as a rule it is the mother who adapts herself to the symbiotic relation, it is usually the father who triangulates. If he succeeds, it will give the child relations both to mother and father, experienced differently and therefore not weighed or played against each other.

This has been studied by various authors. Abelin (1975, 1986), working at the Margaret S. Mahler Institute, developed the notion of early triangulation. If the father is not available much for the child, or the relation between the parents is disordered and the question is which of them has the better links with the child, the latter may feel that it must take sides; there can be no both-and, but only an either-or. The paternal relation is then no complement or enrichment, but a symbiotic alternative. More extreme still is the case when, as here, the father is not there at all.

What reactions become necessary if therefore the boundaries between self and object are not solidly enough established and 'give' under heavy stress? Those who cannot adequately relate to two persons without feeling that they betray either one or the other are bound to run into trouble with regulating their desires for nearness or distance. They are in a specific dilemma already mentioned:

- Since on the basis of their still symbiotic relational needs they cannot easily bear even short intervals without the presence of an object, they must seek relations in which they are closely knit to that object.

- Since at the same time their defective skills at drawing limits easily land them near states of merging, which threatens their ego-identity, they must avoid being too closely linked with the object and seek ways of preventing this.

In the present case, the patient says that he could sever the maternal link only by suicide. Whether that is what his later suicide did perform or whether it expressed a fantasy of merging remains open to question. He had not found the way to his father. That part of himself still behind bars, and so not available to him, he could not make accessible even though his unconscious already knew that it was needed and that the path lay via a third object, namely the father.

During therapy the patient said that he wanted to resume relations with his father, but he did not act on this. On the contrary, when we suggested that he or we should invite the father to a talk, the patient replied evasively: 'Yes, perhaps, but not yet.' Why did we not do it? Had we merely followed the patient's open wish, or had we unconsciously identified with the rest of the family who excluded the father, thus become unwitting fellow actors in a family drama? This we can hardly answer, and certainly not in isolation. A decisive part in treating severe personality disorders is supervision so as to track down our own blind spots, which always have a bearing on therapy.

3

Either/Or
Formations in Relations
at the Borderline Level

In the first transitional domain we see how difficult it is to find the way back from the primary process into the secondary process of daylight, structure, drawing of boundaries, I and thou. One might fall, get lost or lose one's way. Children experience this quite directly and want to know whether they will wake up once they has gone to sleep, whether they will be found when they hide.

Once self and not-self are sufficiently separate, another existential question arises. One can still get lost, though not in the other, but from the other. No longer, 'I have got lost', but 'he has lost me'. The question to be answered is not, 'How securely am I separated from the other?' (pre-psychotic level), but 'How securely am I represented in the other?' (borderline level).

Small children never tire of inventing games in which this question is at stake (I-spy, hide and seek, catching). Freud (1920) observed a game with a wooden reel, which the child threw away and fetched again, to make sure that the passive loss of the mother can always be reversed and even controlled. Children hide in order to be sought and, above all, found. They want to hear stories in which young animals go astray and are recovered. In this way they constantly make sure that the other has an image of them which provokes a feeling of missing them and so will start a search. To most of us it probably matters to know that others have a good image of us. In case of doubt, much will be done to elicit an unambiguous answer. The other need not be extant, but he must have existed at some time. In the primary object, which was once our only and decisive one, we cannot forgo a good image of ourselves. We cannot imagine the desire to live otherwise. If there are doubts here, we try to make the other benevolent and appreciative, sometimes by the use of extreme measures. In fantasies of orphans and of adoption, in the idea of being ill, having an accident, being dead, there is amongst other aspects the question whether there will be somebody to pity or miss us and give us the vital signal of not being indifferent. In suicidal behaviour and suicide, people put their lives at risk to produce that signal.

Precursor of integration: the dream of the two rivers

In the chapter on fusing and anti-fusing suicidal behaviour, we were concerned with forms whose meaning comes from desires of merger and distance and the corresponding fears. Genetically this belongs in the first transitional domain, in which self must separate from not-self. In the course of further development the ability to do this is already at a higher psychic level. At the pre-psychotic level the individual is not yet secure in this and therefore lacks adequate protection against crossing the boundary of fusion in regressive stages. After the second step of differentiation (of separately experiencing self and not-self), the small child already has two ways of interpreting objects and self. Objects can be good or bad (permissive, appreciative, loving; or denying, disapproving, indifferent). Likewise, the subject can see itself as good or bad. Perceiving good and bad features at the same time in one object is irritating and causes fear for good subjective reasons. Consider an example:

> A patient in the first months of her analysis is dreaming that after overcoming many difficulties, in which a man takes her by the hand, accompanies her and says she need not fear persecutors, she finally reaches a canal with silvery white water. On the water there

is a boat in which a man is sitting and rowing slowly. Her companion says: 'At the end of the road we shall meet again.'

Assuming that the companion, or the rower, means me or parts of me, we should indeed meet again at the end of the road along the canal, at a point where the water ends; and would mix with the opposite, a dark and dirty river.

Some years later the river turned up in another dream. The patient reports:

> Around me a desert. On the right and left a river. I am standing between them on a green island. One river is silvery white and clean, the other dark and dirty. In front of me the two want to flow together, but this must not be. I have both hands full trying to keep them apart, but I cannot do it. I am afraid that I shall be inundated. Then you turn up and smile, and my fear vanishes. However, you do not help me to keep the rivers separate and I am annoyed with you.

This dream involves a start with integration. Compared with the beginning of analysis, when there was only one river which was clean (not as yet a canal), a second of opposite quality has appeared. Kernberg (1981) writes that the first object-image occurs in the 'good pole' (the good companion and the clean canal). Only later, when the ego has gained strength, does it dare to take up the negative object pole as well and form an image of it, as occurred in the second dream. The development and strengthening of this patient's ego was reflected in the shape of her dreams. Initial dreams, in which a half-starved baby put in her care could no longer attract attention by screaming, pointed to her giving up libidinous objects; dreams in which skyscrapers have only decrepit staircases, broken or hanging steps and floors, symbolised her desolate inner psychic structure, which could not yet provide the needed regulation for more stable object-relations. In later dreams the houses were being repaired inside, and then she had her own room in one of them, with a table and chair. All this was evidently the result of psychic maturing and structuring, which finally came out in the two-river dream. She could now feel bad features in herself, shown in

ways. For example, the therapist goes away (is bad) only because he sees the patient as bad, of no account and uninteresting. The attending (good) therapist, by contrast, shows by his presence that he regards the patient as good, interesting and lovable.

Constancy of object describes the ability to see, in the reference persons and in oneself, positive and negative sides as features of the same individual. Such an object is 'constant' since the subject need no longer ward off slights by devaluing the object and then dropping it as valueless. Patients who cannot adequately develop more stable and constant relations are easily threatened by loss of objects, in two ways. First, new and freshly idealisable objects must be sought; and second, the inner object-image is harmed, which prevents the object being seen as reliable even if there. Such patients, more than better structured ones, therefore suffer strong fears of losing objects.

Anyone who has worked with suicidal patients knows the ultimacy of the patient–therapist bond. We may thus assume that when object-relations are threatened, suicidal behaviour is the last resort to prevent loss – internally as regards the image, externally between people.

Developing a constant inner object in therapy is equally hard and wearing for patient and therapist, but digesting and integrating the feelings enlisted is an essential part of therapy.

Constancy of object begins in the other

By their approval parents show their child not only that they recognise his individual needs, e.g. hunger, tiredness, the wish to swing or be told a story, but also that they can imagine how all this belongs together and makes the child a whole person. In the course of thus interacting with the child they form a view of his character. They meet him through this constantly developing image. Before the small child can form a self-image, it must have seen that others already have an image of him.

> To a patient who felt me as indifferent, I said that I really took her seriously; but she corrected me and said that I did not perceive her properly, which pointed to something central.

Only when others perceive us do we feel we exist. Only if we see ourselves figured in the other can we form our own self-image, the precondition for becoming a reflective person who discusses with himself. If I experience that the other can have an image of me, I shall be able to develop one of him. I shall be able to conduct with him both an external and an internal dialogue. Since absence of the external object no longer means its non-existence, I shall be able better to cope with it or even desire it. To be on one's own need then no longer mean being abandoned.

A patient remained at home whenever I was on leave. She became afraid to the point of panic. We discovered that she was always keen that I should know where she was. The feeling that I might be unable to trace her caused panic in her. When I was at home she was better able to leave. 'One of us must be on guard.'

In such phases of therapy much of what the patient does can be understood on the basis that it is important to them to create an image of themselves in the other. For example, they might want to give the therapist some real object that he might put on his desk or carry with him. It would be a misunderstanding for the therapist to reject such precursors of an image.

The patient just mentioned who wished that I should know where she was, said of herself:

> I must be able to think of you somewhere on the map or in my head, otherwise I become anxious. I look at the map and quieten down. Otherwise you vanish. The feeling that I could no longer reach you in my head makes me panic. If I do not know where you are, you might be anywhere, and that is too much.

The psychic constancy of the object is still external and geographical. When I asked what would happen if she did not know where I went, she replied:

It would be a shock, I should not understand it. First there would be fear, protest and despair, then exhaustion and total emptiness. Some years ago my fear of your leave was stronger still. It was like a betrayal; no, not that, for I should have been angry and have hated you. That did not happen.

Later things changed. First signs of an object-image that outlasted my absence seem to have been formed. In the last sessions before a leave the patient imagined that for some reason I should not return, because of an accident, falling into a crevasse, breaking a leg. It might look as if this needed primary treatment of the aggression towards the analyst, the negative transference, the wish that I was dead, because I was leaving her. Her further fantasies, however, pointed in another direction: she imagined finding out where I was by telephone and even going there to look me up. Fantasies of an accident served as moving towards the object. She was no longer unable to react to my possible non-return or late return, but could imagine taking action herself. The mood in these pre-leave sessions was now different: fewer fits of panic, but rather regret that I should leave and the pleasure of thinking she might come to visit me. I was sure that her suicidal behaviour would recede, though she often moved at the edge of it; for now she no longer had to give in to being found passive, but could actively come after me.

To vanish in the mass

Part of fearing object-loss is the fear that another will not perceive one as different from other people. One is seen but not recognised. The other is there and nearby, but one is not with him since he cannot distinguish one and so cannot perceive one as a person. Like all others, one is anonymous. Not one among many, perhaps not important but distinguishable and recognisable; but identical with all others, an element in a clone, one of many identical therapeutic twins. If in such phases the patient behaves in ways different from his normal ways, doing something that he assumes others would not do, e.g. taking his coat into the consulting room instead of leaving it in the waiting room, if against his custom he is early or late and wears showy clothes, this might simply aim at being identifiable and recognised by the other. Patients look for a distinguishing mark for the therapist and an identifying aid for themselves. It would be wrong to call this 'acting out'.

One day the patient of the previous section was annoyed that I seemed to work as on a production line, or as in a dovecote. The occasion was that she saw a patient there whom she had not seen before. She entered the room and angrily said to me:

> 'You would not even notice if someone else stood there or if I did not come at all, you have so many patients.' When she had settled down a bit I replied, 'If that is so, it would mean too that I cannot keep up for long the image I have of you, so that it will soon fade.'
>
> *She*: 'That is it, and it leads to your confusing what you hear from one patient with the next one.'
>
> *I*: 'Thus I do not see what makes you the person you are.'
>
> *She*: 'It cannot be other than that in a dovecote or in a mass concern like this one.'
>
> *I*: 'That is how it is here. I must be in the state that you were in your dream of the last session.' (She had dreamt herself in a plane, with below her a vast mass of people all looking alike.)
>
> After a while she said: 'What is odd is that I see this only here. Outside or in a car it is quite different. There I know that you are different, that it is not like that with the many people. But here, everything is confused and I feel that you do not really know who I am.'

It is important to take up anger and decrying tendencies (dovecote, mass concern) in their constructive context: the wish for more social life and for being perceived by another as an unmistakable individual.

To vanish in the mass is not only the fear of being mediocre, an insult to narcissism, but also the self-directed fear of not existing. To be unique is not megalomaniac here, but an essential experience for individuation and a precondition for forming a core identity. 'I am different from others' states a basic feeling needed for individuation. To be rediscoverable, recognisable, translocatable, leaving a trace, all these are descriptions of this basic need. In her last session before her therapist's leave an in-patient hid a marble in her chair. In her first session after the therapist's return she dug between the cushion and the back and recovered the marble. With a smile, she showed it to the therapist and said: 'I am glad it is still there.' (I owe this example to Ruth Müller-Kind.) The patient had left behind a token of herself.

Two forms of object-loss at borderline level

Before turning to suicidal behaviour of the second transitional domain, let me say something about the special fears at this structural level.

Let us return to the picture of the two rivers to be kept apart, the clean and the dirty, or in the usual theoretical terms, the good and the bad images of self and objects. Why was the patient keen to keep them apart, and why did she become afraid when she could not? It is because such a confluence would not yet have led to a new quality of object and self, i.e. to a structure that shows itself as constancy of object. She was afraid that the destruction of the clean river was linked with destruction of the good as such and that her ego would be damaged, that she would inundate everything. Both were threatened: her own good self and her good objects.

At the level of insufficiently integrated positive and negative images of self and objects there is basic insecurity regarding being able to hold on to an object. For one would have to destroy it whenever one finds bad qualities in the other, i.e. one has to devalue the object and turn away from it because it is not as one needs it and as past experience with it has shown. Here we have not just disappointment with the object, since it has as yet no independent qualities attributed to it. It functions still mainly as self-object and only stands in for subject functions.

One of the main functions is constantly to reassure the subject that it is represented as good in the object. If we assume, perhaps somewhat arbitrarily, that there is a self-image of being justified to exist, it is this function that the self-object must take on as long as the subject lacks it. One aim of therapy is to develop this self-image so as to be always available in the subject. If this structure is missing, objects must often be changed; we sometimes overlook that the subject often has no option but to choose another object, since a disappointing object often destroys the feeling of being justified to exist. A new object must be sought to restore this feeling.

The second way of losing an object is via the conviction that if the object sees one's real character, uninteresting and boring yet greedy and full of desires, it will despise one and turn away. Perhaps it will even take to flight, to save itself from the subject's greed. In the extreme case, the subject in its greed can fear that it will destroy the object.

Object relations at this level are therefore beset by constant fears of loss. On the level below (keeping apart self and not-self), the two fears were either to dissolve in the desired object, or, if countermoves are too strong, to lose it (Icarus's dilemma). At the present level the fears concern losing the object because it turns away, being disappointed by one's inferiority; and destroying it (i.e. its inner image), as one became convinced by disappointments that it was unreliable and bad. There are thus two forms of fearing object-loss at this level: passive (being left) and active (withdrawal).

These are merely two sides of the same coin. They determine each other and can quickly switch from one to the other. This is to be expected since they are two forms of reaction of the subject to the same initial process: the object moves of itself.

At this level, the silent process can be subjectively read in only one of two ways: self-devaluation (since I am uninteresting and inferior, the other is right to leave me); or object-devaluation (at bottom I always expected that he would go, he is worthless, cold and mean).

It is not surprising that people whose object relations are mainly tied into this dynamic are easily threatened by fears of object-loss. The reference persons are misperceived and what they do is therefore misread. Correspondingly, the reactions to the object are more or less inappropriate, depending on whether they are guided more by inner or outer reality.

There are many ways (including psychosomatic reactions) for the psyche to react to an imminent loss of object. The next chapter discusses those forms in which suicidal behaviour takes on guiding roles.

4

Suicidal Behaviour between the Borderline Level and the Processes of Integration
(Second Transitional Domain)

On the long path from borderline to constant (integrated) objects and self-images (Klein would say from paranoid-schizoid to depressive) the mechanisms leading to splitting (such as idealisation, denial and devaluation) are increasingly replaced by more mature forms (above all by repression). Clinically, splitting fades out. The interpersonal field of conflict becomes calmer, for instance by more moderate and tolerable super-ego commands that need not be externalised as much as before. However, the increased ego-powers mean greater inner tensions and conflicts. Growing integration of opposing images of self and objects leads to differentiating of inner structure and so creates the psychic preconditions for constancy of objects.

If one pictures the integrating path of the second transitional domain as a continuum, we can discern a pole close to borderline and one close to integration. The first largely lacks scope for constancy of objects and splitting prevails, being experienced syntonically. The second makes it more and more possible to question the validity of images of self and objects obtained by splitting. Splitting becomes ego-dystonic. It may go on for a while in analytic treatment promoting regression, but can be felt as alien in less regressive states, and be viewed and described by the judging ego. It might even be seen as a doubtful bit of the past ('Is that what they say I was?').

As we approach the depressive pole, the products of splitting become less usable, as do the defence mechanisms that alert them. Near the borderline and near integration functions thus connect differently. Let us distinguish between suicidal behaviour near the borderline and near integration.

Suicidal behaviour: manipulative near the borderline; and resignation (ego-syntonic splitting)

The manipulative aspect of suicidal behaviour is probably most widespread and hardest to bear in therapy. Much in evidence is the high intensity of interaction: something is done to one that one can hardly resist. However, if suicidal behaviour shows itself so often and so unconditionally, one must assume that it conceals urgent matters. My observations suggest that object manipulation involves three different but connected goals:

1. securing the object;
2. altering it; and
3. depositing an unbearable aspect of self or objects in another person.

However, the energy for manipulating objects, felt so clearly and concretely in countertransference, is not inexhaustible. Sometimes the patient does not have much primary energy for trying to influence objects. It can then happen that suicidal behaviour, though not fading, no longer shows up in openly manipulative ways. The patient has stopped hoping for success in influencing objects. This is alluded to by the term resignation.

The aim of securing the object (manipulative)

Suicidal behaviour of this type is a sort of hostage-taking. The hostage-taker acts in order to exert pressure on a third person outside the relation. He does not threaten or kill the hostage because it has a special relation to him, but because a third is to be enmeshed in a relation. Unlike murder, hostage-taking involves a largely arbitrary victim. It is not the person that matters, but his role. The target person stands outside the relation between hostage-taker and hostage. Just as in manipulative suicidal behaviour, in which the ego takes the self as hostage: the threat is aimed at the self, but its goal lies outside the relation between ego and self (e.g. in the case of a primary death wish). The threat is aimed at a third person, outside this relation. Just as a hostage-taker tries to manipulate his surroundings in a way that he needs, so does a patient who threatens his self. Clearly this is not a case of murder in the sense of deliberate removal of a certain person. Murder takes place between two persons; suicidal behaviour is triangular, between ego, self and a third. Suicidal behaviour is a scenario in which the ego plays via the bonds of the self (more precisely, bodily self) to reach the thou.

I have earlier shown that a psyche mainly organised on borderline principles is easily hit by fears of object-losses, because the vital structure of object constancy is not yet mature. Objects are only reluctantly recognised as independent, and their way of behaving is still strongly seen as linked with oneself and one's own attractiveness or lack of it. If the object goes away, it is seen as a threat of being left alone, not as a sign that the other has things to do elsewhere: one is not left alone, but abandoned.

If one cannot hold the object by showing oneself as good or interesting (if one were so, the other would not leave), the only way left is control, even by threatening suicide. The aggressive aspect of this expresses the patient's dilemma: it should be treated as not just a menace directed against the self, the primary object. Tabachnick (1961a pp.576–577) stresses that one must not deal with the patient's hostility too early, since that would inflate his guilt feelings. Hostility at first

A long silence follows. Mrs G looks at the ground, with narrow eyes, her forehead wrinkled. Shall I tell him what is going on in me or not? she seemed to ask. What business is it of his? Can I not do what I want? Can I not think and conceal what I want? Then she raises her head, looks me in the eyes and hisses: 'One struggles on and on for nothing!'

I see her on her bicycle, as I often met her when she went to her work experiment and I to the clinic. If it rains, she bends her head into the wind and expends her tough but limited strength. She struggles on. She despises taking a bus.

We get to the time after her discharge and the heap of work that she had planned for home. The long road to the place of training. The impossibility of getting on top of all this had become clear to her the previous weekend when she had gone home to organise certain things. In her flat she had stared at the TV set, which was switched off, and she could not remember anything. It seemed superfluous to turn on the heating. For what?

> *I:* 'A big heap. We had spoken about it last time. I was terrified when I heard of the load you were going to shoulder.'

She grinned. 'I cannot see why you want to kill yourself.' Then it becomes clearer. Bitterly she says: 'If my father hears that I failed, he will have a good laugh.'

> *I:* 'Will he? Why, how does that come in?'

> *Mrs G:* 'All these years I have tried to learn a profession from which I can live. That was my only wish. If now my father finds out that I have not managed to do that he will tell himself: "I have always said that she is not worth investing another penny in."'

> *I:* 'The struggle between you and your father is still going strong.'

Mrs G utters a bitter and despising grunt, looking to the ground, again with hard lips, narrow eyes and a wrinkled forehead.

After a while I ask: 'Why do you think you have the right to expect to master all this: your training, working at night and perhaps some written homework? Does one have to manage all this?'

Mrs G, after thinking a while, says: 'One must manage, others do.'

I: 'So you cannot confront your father if you fail. What about yourself?'

She keeps silent. Then she suddenly replies: 'Would you agree if I were to leave tomorrow?'

I am amazed and say: 'Leave? Go home?'

Mrs G: 'Yes.'

I: 'No, of course not.'

Mrs G: 'Not even if I sign a paper saying that the decision was mine?'

I: 'No, not even then.'

A long and stubborn silence follows. After a while I say: 'You will not get rid of me so easily.'

Mrs G: 'How stupid.'

I: 'I should be able to say at last I am rid of Mrs G, a lucky escape, I am not responsible even if something happens to her, since I have her signature.'

Mrs G: 'Yes, roughly like that.'

I: 'But your signature does not free me from responsibility; I do not want to shed it anyway.'

Mrs G looks at me in amazement as if she is about to cry. Then, leaning slightly back, with smaller eyes, tight lips and wrinkled brow she hisses bitterly at me: 'In that case the whole business will be delayed by a few weeks' (discharge had been planned for a few weeks later).

I: 'Now you are giving something back to me.'

She has to smile and says: 'I do not want anybody to care about me.'

I: 'You seem rather to want to lean on me.'

She grins and says: 'Maybe.'

A longer silence follows. After a while I ask her: 'How is the sore on your leg?'

Mrs G: 'Not too bad.'

I: 'Has this been replaced by a sore inside here?' (I am pointing to my chest) 'and when you say you would sign a paper that you are leaving at your request, do you open the wound again as it were?'

Mrs G: (after a while) 'Yes, perhaps so.'

I: 'We should discuss this further.'

She says nothing. I mention the suicide pact: 'How is it, can you report if the other side gets the upper hand again, the side with which you want to harm yourself?'

Mrs G: 'Yes, I think so.'

We take leave.

Whether this conversation, which struck me as positive, was effective as an intervention in a crisis is hard to assess. Presumably the patient had felt understood, but this had probably involved the danger of too near an approach.

The following day during my visit she sat in a dangerous position on the window ledge. This she had often done before, but this time the duty doctor was afraid she might really jump, and had pulled her quickly back into the room. She made it plain that she was in danger and we put her into a different clinic which had a closed ward. After discharge, she wrote to us and told us about her professional plans and that she was reasonably well. With regular discharge she would have reached home about the same time, but she had to undergo a period of being forcibly pushed out in order to master the separation. She was still unable to move away from proximity in a good way. Too many desires would be aroused that she seemed unable to guide, because she did not know their extent. It was safer to feel expelled and rejected, and compel the object that had given her good things to behave so that she could be felt pushed out. Only from a distance could she resume a positive contact with it.

Goal of changing the object: the meaning of representing a good object

In my view the wish expressed in suicidal behaviour consists in changing an object, not in dying. The intention is aimed at the object, not at the self. The self might even envisage its own death in order to attain the prior aim of changing the object. We shall try to show why and when this is seen as prior. What is involved is evidently a function of the object, without which life is impossible.

We recall Freud's statement that no neurotic wants to kill himself if this wish is not diverted from another target onto oneself (Freud 1916, p.438). As regards the direction of the the suicidal intention, we agree: the ultimate goal is an object. On what is to be done to it, my view is the opposite of Freud's: he starts from the assumption that the object is to be killed (which would occur via introjection into the subject intending this). However, in my experience much favours the assumption that the object is not to be killed, but changed. An indifferent and dismissive object is to become congenial and friendly, or 'empathic', as Rohde-Dachser (1986) has called it in connection with masochist episodes. The two theses complement each other. They reside on different levels: killing the object is on a more archaic level, changing it is on a maturer one. 'I will not let thee go except thou bless me', Jacob said when struggling with the angel (Genesis 32:26). Only when the angel takes notice of him, perceives him and by a blessing proves that he regards him as worth it (and not to be repudiated), can Jacob let go.

The picture of the struggle with the angel leads into the area of change of object, the second goal of manipulation. At stake is the certainty that the other stays not from compulsion but from volition. The ultimate goal of suicidal behaviour, which shows itself in object manipulation, is to hold the other, to change him and make him 'good', which means creating in him a good image of oneself. Thus viewed, the creator's seeing that his creation was good is the decisive formula for preserving the object. The words 'let there be' created the object; the assessing formula endows it with the right to exist and last. Kohut's omnipotent object must be able to utter it along with the creation of his subject, to secure the latter's existence. If the subject does not feel itself thus assessed, it will not be able to live. If the patient does not see his therapist regarding him as 'good', therapy cannot have 'good' effects on him. As long as the psyche lacks a self-image that justifies its existence, as the formula from Genesis does, it will not be able to live by its own power. Seen in this way, the external object is indeed omnipotent, feeding not on its various abilities that are so much greater than those of the dependent subject, but on its power favourably to assess the latter.

The proposition of the sentence: 'And he saw that it was bad' would be lethal at once. The subject is as yet not an individual largely independent of the omnipotent object, and therefore would have to die, perhaps in the hope of being created afresh with a favourable assessment and so able to be released into independent life.

Many patients with suicidal behaviour seek such an object that guarantees existence and can be made to issue the favourable formula. A repudiator is to become an acceptor. He is to give a blessing and thereby show that he wishes one to live. If he does not, the only hope is for repentance, blessing after death. The other is to regret his neglect of the dependent subject, regret being indifferent to its life or death. Death by suicide is to arouse a positive feeling in the other after all. Since life without assurance of such a feeling is impossible, death can be given a meaning which provides justification in retrospect: if one is missed, one must have lived. However, since the other at present repudiates, or seems to, having no voluntary positive feelings for one, he has to be forced to have them. If this shows up in transference, the therapist will inevitably appear as rejecting the patient. Only then does the patient–therapist relation reach the critical point where the patient's actions (including suicidal behaviour) can become a turning point. This dangerous stretch has to be crossed. The rejected subject, by behaving suicidally or even killing itself, hopes to make the object good, or at least leave an ineradicable trace to create the preconditions for being itself able to live.

Reading psychoanalytic views on suicide from the early 1900s, as summarised by Federn (1928/29), one notes that this perspective is not all that new. That one cannot live without feeling loved was recognised by various analysts. Sadger (Federn 1928/29, p.339) says that life is given up only by one who had to give up the hope of being loved. Freud (1923, p.288) asserts that the fear of death in melancholia allows only one explanation: the ego gives itself up because it feels that the super-ego hates and persecutes it. For the ego, to live is the same as to be loved by the super-ego, which fulfils the same protective and saving function as the father previously, and providence or fate later.

Klemann (1983, p.119), in his research on early childhood experiences of suicidal patients, states that they were not only often hit by object-losses and separations, but experienced these as threatening life. Such a child will find it hard to develop a super-ego that will love it, as Freud demands, so that it can see itself as wanted and worth being alive. However, in Freud's time one would hardly see suicide itself as an attempt to bring about such a favourable object, at the risk of one's life, so to speak. Because of the then current theory of murder on the introjected object, there may have been no room for this approach.

Freud then starts from the notion that in order to live one needs a loving inner structure, and puts it into the super-ego. If later Kohut (1973) speaks of the mirroring self-object, it is something rather similar: an object as yet external in the development of the child has certain qualities and can therefore fulfil certain tasks. It loves the child as someone becoming detached, whom it can therefore perceive and confirm, by reflecting the child's behaviour to him and thus showing that it has perceived him.

The notion of 'mirroring' has been adopted, but is not very appropriate, because it reduces the wealth of the total process to a somewhat arid idea. For what this object does goes much further than mere mirroring. It is a comprehensive absorption. The object shows that it perceives the child as a whole and in its various qualities and peculiar points. It shows itself glad about what the child is doing. It not only mirrors the child's behaviour to him but supports him with its own positive reaction, and so encourages him to continue doing what he is doing, namely growing and developing himself. Such an empathic mirroring object shows the child that there are powers in him that develop in a good way and, indeed, that he is that power. The child is to learn not that he has, but that he is.

Small children are inventive in developing games in which they prepare some food for the parents. Small stones, leaves, buttons, whatever is available, are carefully prepared and served. The child needs the experience that the parents symbolically consume something that the child has produced. If they say that it is tasty, they assert that the child has the power to produce something good. By eating it, they absorb it and so give it a place, quite concretely and physically at first, and so let it become an image. Children give their parents what they find and show them what they can do. They expect the parents to see this and so make sure that they all live in the same world. They wait for an encouraging word and thus daily reassure themselves of the other having a good image of them, which in a second step they must build up in themselves. The Creator's judgement, 'And he saw that it was good' has constantly to be repeated by parents to their children. It is not a single valuation of the product, but a constant confirmation of the process of development.

By these processes the core self builds itself. Later, when a maturer ego perceives and assesses it, this enables it to reply: 'That is how I am.' Unfavourable conditions for the core self to develop can show up as identity disorders. One is unsure who and how one really is, which can lead to a desperate search. However, one cannot find oneself: 'that is how I am' is a formula leading nowhere. All we find is what others have said about us. This disorder seems to be linked to the omnipotent object at the time never having looked for or found one.

The empathic object, which at first is external, is gradually taken up into the child's self and becomes an inner structure. If in development such an external object is lacking, then no matching inner structure that might break away from an outer prototype can adequately develop. One must then rely more than others on some external object. In terms of the psychology of self and object-relations, Rohde-Dachser (1986) here speaks of an 'empathic object', and in her study on the psychodynamics of masochist fantasies describes how such patients impressively seek to create such an object. In the struggle for empathy, the object is 'suffered into existence', as she puts it.

Destructive and constructive suicidal motives; the case of Fritz

We can amplify on Federn's thesis that only someone whom another wants dead kills himself (1928/29, p.388) by adding that by his own death he wants to transform the other's wish for death into one for life.

We give here an extract form a case described by Bernfeld (1928/29). The case is described entirely in terms of a death wish directed against the self after it was aimed at the loved and hated object, so that the emphasis was on destructive suicidal motivation.

Fritz, 19 years old, is under protective supervision in an apprentice-ship in a blacksmith's workshop in the country. He urges his parents and the supervisor to let him return home and change his training. As till now he had been highly unstable, this request is not granted. The fight had lasted over six months when Fritz responded to a letter from his mother by trying to gas himself on 23 December 1923. The attempt failed, as did a further one the following night. Before the deed he wrote farewell letters to his parents and which he did not destroy even after he decided to live on. He fantasised them into a diary in letter form, finishing on 14 May 1924 with an inner reconciliation with his parents. In a letter to Fritz, his mother writes: 'Your father regrets that he was not stricter with you and relied on the good core in you. Now he wants to jump out of his skin when you send such letters. We know life there is not too nice, but a man of character will face up to the mess he has got into.'

The father, once an omnipotent object, regrets that he had counted on the son's good core. Fritz desperately tries to be accepted nevertheless. In his last farewell letter he writes: 'Dearest parents, do not grieve about me. If only you had seen what I needed. Could you ever have thought, especially you, dear father, that I am of your blood, your only son on whom in your heart you place your hopes, in whom you see your own youth again, could you have imagined that I would give up my training three times merely for fun, because of a whim or dream? ... What I needed, what made me ill, was my spiritual hunger, which I could not satisfy ... I have collapsed under the force and weight of my hatred. Test me and yourself, dear father, I am your true son, and you could have been proud of me ... Dear parents, love your two girls all the more ... Be happy and finally accept the last greeting from your son.'

Unlike Jacob, who attained the blessing of the angel, Fritz in his diary obtains no such blessing, and he makes several attempts at suicide. That he failed is perhaps an accident. Had he died it would have been because there was nobody left to see the good core in him, and he himself was as yet psychically too weakly protected to attain by himself the power residing in the blessing. The issue of the drama was, however, that the episode could be ended by reconciliation with the inner parental images. No real exchange with the parents ever occurred afterwards.

The fantasy of violent suicide

For many years, Mrs R had the fantasy of suicide by jumping from a skyscraper or running into a speeding car on the motorway. During her stay in a clinic these fantasies developed into suicidal impulses which were in urgent need of being transformed. The patient helped herself by avoiding the nearby motorway and the higher storeys of the clinic. At times we had to transfer her to a closed ward for a few days.

Why and when is suicidal behaviour fantasised in this way? What is the difference between this and suicide, or ideas of it, in the fusing mode with the idea of dissolving in an infinitely good object? In my view it is that such an object does not exist. Therefore a merging suicide attempt cannot be imagined. With whom should one merge? However, the troubled psyche does not give up. If there is no good object, one can try to create one. If other means have failed, one's own death might achieve something. This goal is one reason for violent suicide. Falling off a skyscraper, driving into a bridgehead, the fantasy of running into a car, these are forms of suicide that extremely disfigure the body. What could thus far not be conveyed or seen, now becomes unmissable through a bodily change. One does not merely walk towards a train, but this train is the significant other against whom one throws oneself in order to feel something, which he otherwise seems not to do. Something must be triggered in him that remains, even if it is a permanent injury. Violent suicide means readiness to risk one's own body in order to provoke in the other a process that will lead him to have an image of us. One patient called it being posthumously shifted. If one is missed, it would show that the other valued one after all. It seems essential to have somebody who can accept how one feels, because he has an image of me and he wants to do so because he loves or values me. Here the body seems less important.

Graveside regrets

'Mummy give me a little horse' is the title of a seemingly harmless sentimental song, once often heard in request programmes on the air. A child wants a little horse from his mother but she cannot give it to him. She is desolated and grieves to death. The hearse to the cemetery is drawn by two horses. Now the child grieves: that was not the sort of horse he wanted, and too late he regrets the wish that killed his mother. This horror song suggests that good children should have no wishes, because against their children's wishes mothers are defenceless. The mother, by her death, forces the child's regret. (Reference to this song was given me by Dr Burgemeister. My thanks to her.)

In the analysis of Mrs E, suicidal tendencies over a long period played a big role. The psychodynamics of her suicidal behaviour changed as her therapy brought progress. At first the suicidal behaviour was hardly noticeable – she had only weakly occupied her objects and thus was not in a position to express dangers, let alone to make demands. As her images of self and objects improved, her suicidal tendencies became markedly more manipulative. She therefore asked for more sessions and exerted pressure on me, partly with suicidal tendencies, a favourable prognostic sign if seen as an incipient revival of libidinous objects. Later, in a fantasy of graveside regret, she was able to describe a further aspect of her suicidal ways. She approached this topic via a dream in which she stands near a precipice, safe from falling because secured by a rope. Behind her stand two men and she tells herself that she should really be afraid and concerned about them and should hold on to them. 'I wanted someone to hold me,' she said, 'though that was not necessary since I was secured.'

> She remembered earlier precipice dreams in which she was afraid to fall or actually fell, waking up shortly after hitting the ground.
>
> She said: 'I do not know who the two men were. They were not you!'
>
> *I*: 'You rather emphasise it.'
>
> *Mrs E*: 'Previously you were always there in such dreams.'
>
> I said, 'Perhaps I am no longer as essential now,' but realised that I had said it too soon without knowing what the problem was. Somewhat too sure of myself, I had hoped that she wanted to talk about her becoming more independent of me.
>
> Mrs E was silent. After a while she said seriously: 'Do not take the chance. If you think that I no longer need you, it is still too risky.' She thus warns me not to expect too much from her growing independence and inner maturity. She seemed to say I should not demand too much at once. I remembered her earlier dreams of

derelict skyscrapers with crumbling stairs and ceilings; in the last year the dream houses had become more solid inside.

I: 'Perhaps it would be risky. Still, the risk might now be less of falling, as earlier. It might in a way be risky as well to be able to secure oneself better. Others need not then be on hand at once, which makes them look more indifferent and less caring about one.'

Mrs E: 'In that case I might as well jump.' After a pause she goes on: 'I do not know whether I would jump to die or to tell you off and repay you out of anger because you have treated me so badly.'

I: 'Perhaps I am to regret something.'

Mrs E: 'I always wished that you would regret having mis-understood me, that you did not see what I was worth. And I always hoped that when I am dead you would, and be sorry that you preferred the other patients. That you had them at all was enough for you to misunderstand me time and again.'

The certainty that one will be held back by the other at the decisive moment is an important experience. Without it genuine steps towards individuation and separation are hard to visualise, since the danger is that one jumps into a vacuum, or, as another patient symbolised fears of losing objects, you would drift out to sea without a safety rope. Distance is friendly only when you can return, and that you can only do if you are sure that someone with whom there is a link awaits you on shore. If the link is not to break even if the real object is no longer there, one has to make do with its image.

Suicide as consequence of abandoning the object (resignation)

If one fails to manipulate the object into change, resignation may follow, and little trace of the earlier dramatic suicidal behaviour may be noticeable even though it might still be there. On the contrary, such a patient can still be in danger from that behaviour, not now for gaining an object, but from a feeling of indifference whether one lives or not. One patient could not do much with the question whether she could comment on why she no longer wished to live. Her logical answer was: 'I am not so much concerned about whether I want to live or not. There were times when I wanted to kill myself, and wanted that others should notice and think about it. Nor is it that I no longer want to live. That does not apply. The point is that I no longer have to live.'

This patient has given up the wish of an object viewing her positively and has even let it go internally. A patient with suicidal behaviour aimed at securing or changing an object neither could nor would have to put it like that, since he still hopes he can hold and attach the object through his own power. This hope no longer exists in one who says he need no longer live.

Such patients can no longer demand what they urgently need. We must beware of inferring that there is no emergency merely because there are no appeals, though at times the emergency is hard to grasp. Whether it is not there or merely not reported can perhaps be distinguished via countertransference.

How can one infer, from one's own feelings about and reactions to a patient, that he is in some danger, when he himself hardly mentions it directly? In connection with countertransference we shall consider the therapist's state of feelings called constellation of the abandoned object (Kind 1986). The therapist feels that the patient has abandoned him: the therapist has become superfluous and of no value to the patient. At the peak of this process the therapist feels superfluous as such. How does the therapist come to see himself like this? For it was the patient who spoke of himself as superfluous and useless. The concept of projective identification tries to answer this: in interacting with the other, one's own states of feeling can be induced in him. In the therapeutic setting, taking the patient as the source, they can show up in the therapist's countertransference. However, we must be cautious in using this explanatory principle. It is rather easy to say, 'I feel this and that, therefore the patient has triggered this in me,' when one has in fact neglected one's own weak points.

If one considers countertransference while taking one's own conflicts into account, it becomes clear that the patient non-verbally helps to create the therapist's feeling of being abandoned precisely because he does not interact. The therapist now feels the same way as the patient, or similarly. By projective identification the patient has called forth in the therapist a state corresponding to an aspect of the patient's self or resembling one of his inner objects. He has transported something into the therapist. It is now the therapist's turn to start something that the patient can no longer do. The therapist can tell himself that this is the patient's way of conveying his feelings.

This is noticeable most clearly when a once noisy and highly interactive manipulative sort of suicidal behaviour fades, and the patient no longer speaks of it, although there are no signs that his state has improved. The feeling of being spell-bound disappears, one feels somewhat freer at first, but at the same time it is clear that the patient has not only relaxed his grip but has let one go. Collaboration and suicide pact, a continued topic of therapeutic discussion in manipulative securing of the object, seem no longer to bind patient to therapist.

If, in such transitional stages from securing to giving up an object, there is intervention by the apparent new relaxation and the therapist's regained freedom of action, the latter's hopelessness, doubt and the other feelings mentioned, then the abandoned object may threaten the patient via projective identification. (We may of course ask whether resignation is correctly included in the second transitional domain or whether it might not belong to the fusing forms of the first transitional domain. This may well be so in the individual case. It is mentioned here because in cases from my observation there are no adequate signs of a destabilised subject–object boundary.)

The object destroyed and restored

Working through various situations of disappointment with other people and myself, Mrs E calmly looked back: 'Whenever you disappoint me, for example when you attend a congress or go on leave, I conduct a systematic campaign to annihilate you. I run through all the good experiences with you, when you have helped me, everything I value in you, and smash them systematically. I tell myself that you help me only to be able to show a successful analysis, or to earn money, or to avoid greater difficulties if I make no progress, and you do not want this because it would be troublesome. I go on in this way until nothing good is left and I have a totally bad image of you. This is a dangerous state, for it would then seem reasonable to kill myself. Such a person does not deserve a patient who develops, he merits only one who fails. I then imagine killing myself to show you how badly you have treated me. Somehow that makes me feel better, I no longer feel that I am considered so worthless by you.'

This clearly showed some progress in that the campaign against her image of me did not have to be automatically carried through; she could recognise the impulse as it arose, in the form of an insult, and she was able to speak about it. She no longer had to deny that she could move independently of me, her ego had become strong enough to perceive reality more accurately. She did, however, often interpret my plans and acts that were independent of her as directed against her. She then asked herself what was going on, since I was otherwise always there for her, seemed to have no other patients and no obligations. Such situations had of course always existed, but not been felt so much as affronts, since an adequate denial of reality had protected her from this. The fact that she now saw independent moves of her therapist, though still via insult, pointed to a growth of her ego: it mattered to her. She was no longer indifferent to whether I had to deal with her or with someone else. She began to see her objects in terms of libido – a clear advance on the inarticulate half-starved baby.

However, a serious setback occurred. The object to which one entrusted oneself, from whom for the first time one wanted something thus showing that one loved it, this object shows itself indifferent. It simply leaves. One must realise that this form of object relation is still quite one-sided and is seen as such by the subject without reflection.

Balint (1951, p.138) describes object relations at this point, in his essay on love and hate, stating that the original object relation is one in which only one partner can make demands, the other being treated as an object, though as one of instinct or love. In case of disappointment, hate supervenes. Balint comments that to hate we must first depend on the persons or objects concerned, for hate measures inequality between object and subject; the smaller this inequality and the more mature the object, the less we need hate (p.142).

Hate was used by my patient for initiating destruction of the good aspects of the object. This was necessary to stabilise her damaged feeling of self-worth. The black and white rivers wanted to merge and the former seemed to extinguish the latter. Here she felt fear. She saw that she could not solve her problem in this way, since the object on which she still depended and which she needed for further development would be extinguished (subjectively, i.e. its image). She had only two ways to avoid this dilemma. She could try to restore the object to its previous pure and wholly good form, keeping the two rivers apart, but falling back into idealised relations of dependence on objects. Or she could try to take the arduous path of recognising objects as entities with their own rights, as Winnicott (1971, pp.101–110) has put it; in that case she would be protected from experiencing the other's independent moves as directed against her. The patient continues: 'If I have made everything I value in you bad and nasty, if now I only hate you and could kill myself to pay you back, then I become afraid and tell myself that I am not really sure whether you are quite as indifferent to me. Then I bring together everything positive about you that I can find. The trouble is that I do not know how you really are.'

The patient clearly describes that she cannot yet have ambivalent feelings which relate to the one but do not exclude the other, that she is still in a 'pre-ambivalent stage', as Abraham (1924) has put it. Later in her analysis, Mrs E was able to stop in time, in her inner campaign against good aspects of the object, and so able to avoid the dangerous state of totally emptying her inner objects. In this context we came to mention an early childhood memory of hers. She rode down a steep hill on her bicycle and could not brake but merely held on. She fell and was seriously injured. This memory had been known for some time during the analysis, but I had always assumed that the brakes were faulty. Closer inquiry showed that there were brakes but the child was at the time not yet able to use them properly.

Now she was able to stop the inner campaign against the good image of the therapist and to brake. When I said: 'In contrast with then, you can now brake when you want to,' she replied: 'That is new. Before, I simply surged ahead.' She notices that she is better able to deal with offending remarks and not as much in need of retiring from the other as before. Summing up, the patient described her development in this phase of analysis with the processes of translocation, annihilation and restitution of the object roughly thus:

> It is reassuring to know where you are, for example at the weekend. I then imagine where your car is and what you are doing. In this way I keep in touch. If I do not know where you are, there is a danger that you will be lost to me. My fantasy roams about looking for you, but can never be sure where you are. I think I have never yet seriously missed anyone. I have missed certain things that I have done with someone, going out to eat, to the pictures, cooking, but not really the person.

> In the past I was unable to look after myself properly; perhaps I really could, but I did not care how I was, whether I was cold or hungry.

> Do I really know people? I soon recognise their weak points and tricks, but I do not really know them, and do not really accept their strong points and what they positively amount to. I do not want to see what I might envy in others.

> In the past I simply wrote off people when I was offended. For me they were dead. With you it was also like that, and I told myself I did not need you. That is a dangerous moment, when I leave nothing good in you.

The course is always the same:

- You disappoint me, which for me shows that I do not mean anything to you.

- Then I am desperate, and that is worse than anger.

- Then I remember all the incidents when you were nasty, and less and less of good remains in you.

- In the end I become afraid, and notice why: because you would no longer exist if I go on like that.

- Then I try to revive the good experiences with you, quickly before it is too late.

- When within I have nearly wiped you out, I have to call you to strengthen the other side. Otherwise I might lose my self-control and something uncontrollable happens: 'I' do not act, 'it' acts using me.

Do I like people? Yes, some, but I can leave them in a trice, if I am disappointed in them.

I am amazed at all the things I managed to bear with you. Another could not have done a fraction of what you have done to me.

Why I have put up with it? I do not know, it is puzzling. Perhaps it was the requirement not to break off the analysis. Reason came to my help and told me that you are not only nasty. I recalled occasions when you were not. My head told me to stay. Besides, there was the splendid feeling of revenge: some time I shall kill myself, and then you will see.

Did my vengeful feelings save me? No, it was only ever phoning you that has saved me. When I phoned I had no feelings of revenge, but felt that I could no longer brake and had to destroy my good image of you. This happened always when I could leave not a shred of good in you. But revenge also somehow helped me. At least there was the feeling that there is someone on whom I can take revenge, so that there exists a person.

However, there were other moments when you were no longer
properly there. Then disappointment was even worse, since not
even revenge was possible, and the only need was to be gone.

Suicidal behaviour from resignation goes beyond anger and revenge. It
results from experience that not even anger and revenge are not
sufficient response to. This develops into an extreme detachment of
inner object images. This state, which is mirrored in the therapist as the
countertransference of being abandoned, is the bottom of the valley
from which the patient can no longer escape unaided. He then has to
rely on the therapist actively approaching him, even if he does not
appear openly suicidal. He does not appear so because he can no longer
hint at this desolate situation of his, or because he would regard such a
hint as pointless. This bottom of the valley is the state of the abandoned
object. It is now more than ever the therapist's task to hold the relation.
If libidinous images for objects begin to stir, suicidal behaviour
becomes more noticeable again. In that case one can breathe again, even
though therapeutic interaction becomes more difficult and exhausting.

Suicide near integration in depression
(ego-dystonic splitting)

In forms of suicidal behaviour in the second transitional domain, we
have so far dealt only with types that could be considered against a
background of self and objects in their antithetical aspects. Near the
borderline, pole splitting is still largely felt as ego-syntonic. However,
this is not so near the integrative pole. In the ego-syntonic case, the
question whether the object could be experienced differently does not
even arise. This becomes possible only near integrative processes. Then
one can feel more often that one may have misunderstood the object,
that one has idealised it by neglecting its negative features. So one is
able to ward off being angry at disappointment or devaluing and
rejecting it, and can stabilise self-worth feelings and is able to leave it;
although this involves setting up an idealised object in another person.
An average object would be empty and therefore once again bad.

If in the course of therapy one gradually leaves the borderline level, suicidal forms of behaviour residing there lose their function. Not that integration can skip critical phases. On the contrary, one does not always realise what turbulence arises in the patient at this stage. He has to master the task of introducing quite new aspects into his self and into his object-images, modifying existing ones without entirely losing them. At levels near borderline, objects are exchanged; here they must be transformed. If this evokes suicidal behaviour, one must see it in its different context. Mostly it is no longer of the forms described before, but of a new quality where guilt feelings play a bigger role than earlier. Hence my term integrative suicidal behaviour in depression – a bit heavy but clearly pointing to the therapeutic phase concerned.

> With a patient admitted to a ward, his disappointments led to a talk with me that illustrates the work of modification just described. I had wrongly given him a date when I was otherwise engaged, and he was indignant: I had failed either because I was absent-minded, excusable because of my work-load; or because I had deliberately tested him. In the following conversation he cannot decide how to take it – in either case he feels uncomfortable. My behaviour had more than annoyed him. He is reminded of an aggressive animal from a dream. I asked who the owner might be.
>
> *He:* (laughs) 'You mean it is mine because the dream was?'
>
> *I:* 'Perhaps, but it may be someone else's. Mine or another's.'
>
> *Patient:* 'Perhaps it belongs to my boss, who is chasing me from my post because he has someone else.'
>
> *I:* 'How would you take the idea that in each of the three there might be such a biting animal, in your boss, in you and in me?'
>
> *Patient:* 'Not in me! Or perhaps in me too? I can be quite cutting and aggressive at times.' He keeps quiet for a while and then goes on: 'Not in you. At least I do not want such a thing in you against me. No, you are not like that. Or have you some of this too?'
>
> *I:* 'I rather think I have, that I can bite and become aggressive.'
>
> *Patient:* (hesitatingly) 'I do not know.'

I: 'And if it were like that?'

Patient: 'Somehow I feel ill at ease with this idea, but if I see you like that in the ward, it could be so. You are at times quite short and can turn acid.'

I: 'Yes, sometimes I am.'

Patient: 'Perhaps it is because of the trouble caused you by patients.'

I: 'Then it would once more be because of you, and not really in me. Is that more pleasant?'

Patient: 'Somehow clearer, and less frightening, but it cannot be quite right.'

The patient became reflective. If I had sides like that, he had to change his image of me. If, however, I somehow managed to deal with such sides, he need no longer fear being too aggressive, but could use this more constructively to his own advantage.

Take away the splitting mechanism, and it is no longer so clear-cut how I am or how the other is. The antithetical images of self and objects for Dr Jekyll and Mr Hyde, hitherto kept sufficiently apart, come closer together and seem mutually to cede qualities. This gradually brings out the outline of the person of whom each is a partial aspect.

However, this coming near has problems. Kernberg (1978, p.296) points out that the patient has to face a highly difficult emotional situation at the decisive moment: he must now admit the real good parts of the analyst or mother which he had so far denied and devalued, and so expose himself to an immense feeling of guilt because of his earlier aggression against the analyst. Many a patient will be desperate at having time and again despised and treated inconsiderately the analyst, and indeed all people who have become important to him in life; sometimes he becomes convinced that he has destroyed all those he might have loved or who might have loved him.

> The night staff reported that a patient had sat on the banisters on the second floor, sliding down in a dangerous manner. Moreover, she had taken uncontrolled amounts of potassium, to make up loss

due to vomiting, as she put it. During the visit next day the ward doctor and I mentioned this to her and said we were worried and would therefore search the room; and we would consider how better to protect her. The talk was urgent and direct.

In the evening she was missing from the ward. She did not return till late. The duty doctor reported that she had felt ashamed in her talk with the ward doctor and myself earlier in the day. She had noticed how bad she was for kicking those who cared for her and wanted to help.

When we talked the following morning she told us that recently she had been suffering during normal contact with others. She would push them away. I asked whether care by others sometimes comes too close. She said yes, and I replied that pushing away is a vital ability to shift the other to the right distance, but possibly painful as well if one actually wanted to do it differently.

The work of integration can be critical for various reasons, and can lead to suicidal behaviour. With increasing tolerance for the other's psychic reality the patient loses subjective grounds for his hostility. This can revive the splitting mechanism and an experience of mainly negative parts of the self, and lead to critical self-accusation. Here one must show the patient the constructive aspect of his hostility; e.g. the implicit foiled desire for a good object.

In treating borderline patients we reach the point where depression is born. With growing integration of opposite images of self and objects one comes to assess the other more realistically and thus be able to empathise with him. The patient then recognises that his attacks on the therapist do not leave the latter indifferent, but can upset, annoy or offend; indeed, that the therapist cares about dangers and welcomes growth. Parallel to acquiring the power to empathise, guilt and regret appear. For the first time the patient experiences grief where previously there was depression.

The patient who had expressed fear of integration in the dream of the two rivers describes this phase of therapy thus: 'Something has changed. Something is happening in me.' She reports that she would like to come with me on my impending trip, that my car had a dent, that the child's seat was unsafe, that I looked different today, more relaxed. She is considering how I am, worries and reflects what my other activities might be. She begins to develop empathy, which presupposes greater distance linked with greater independence from her self-object. Then she considers what therapy has brought her and observes that she feels grateful towards me, though she also had greatly suffered during therapy from all the frustration that she had experienced through me.

Patient: 'I have both feelings in me.'

I: 'Perhaps what is new is that you can now have them both together at the same time.'

Patient: 'I used to have only one of the two, which was much harder and more taxing. But it was clearer too. Either I was terribly angry with you, or I found you splendid. Now I no longer know how I am to find you. I still find you good, but sometimes I think that you are rather one-sided in what you do, and wonder whether I am not also disappointed by you. I want to push this thought aside, but know that there is something in it. This makes me somehow helpless.'

I: 'Do the two rivers merge at present, the silvery white one and the dark one?'

The patient: (in a sad voice) 'I do not know, perhaps.' After a while: 'If only I had not come today.'

The depressive position is the phase of development of new affects, in which the ability to grieve (instead of suffering depression) and gratitude (instead of envy) play vital roles (Melanie Klein 1957). It is like the merging of two rivers.

In the depressive position, old names and old states of ego and objects must be given up in favour of new perspectives and new forms of experience. The confluence of two rivers produces a third thing, but they have to change their previous form.

In a later dream the patient returned to the topic of integration. In her first such dream, the confluence of opposite streams frightened her because of the danger of being swamped. However, it looked otherwise in the following dream:

> I am in an old half-decayed truck. It is empty and I have a couch in one corner. Then I see that the door is wide open and I climb out and stand in a station with many tracks. Many people stand on the platform and say that the last train is leaving over there. They all move there to catch it, and I go too.

She remembered the trucks of the transports to concentration camps, and the life not worth living. I reminded her of her own earlier assessment of herself as something for whom the world had no use.

If one misses the last train, one is left alone on the platform. The patient remembered the last sessions in which we mentioned that in the course of analysis she had socially isolated herself more and more. Now she noticed that this was not really so any longer. People called her again, not least, as it turned out, because she answered the telephone when it rang. Her life was no longer worthless and she was able to face people on the phone again. She said: 'I go to the phone when it rings. Before, I used to let it ring, if I felt bad. I did not want to impose myself on others.'

The doors of the truck were open and she was allowed to leave the dark and empty container of her rejected self with the destructive goal. She dared to enter a world in which there were others who were quite normal. She noticed that her goals were the same as theirs and went with them. She was no longer afraid to sink in the mass. She noticed that, unlike previously, she no longer depended on every possible contact. She could be more selective because she was better able to be alone.

In the dream of the two rivers the point of integration (the beginning of the depressive position) is symbolised by the merging of opposite streams. In this second dream it comes out again in the image of the truck, on a higher level. Here, too, there are two opposite elements: the couch in the dark corner and the open door. In the first dream it was an image to which the patient reacted with fear, having to fight against the imminent new structures. Now she develops an image that shows that a new way is open to her.

The door of the truck, separation between rejected self and the world turned towards life, can remain open. The patient does not try to shut it. Both aspects of self are allowed to know of each other.

Mrs E had regained the self that once she sought to destroy. She did not have to have it killed or kill it herself for reasons of worthlessness. This part of the self had recovered the vital feeling of being worth living. The suicidal behaviour that originally served to change the object had lost its function, because the self had changed, the patient no longer behaved suicidally. The function of the external object (to accept the subject) had become an inner structural element, so that the patient herself could regulate this. It was thus not surprising that she, who had been unable to imagine ending her analysis, now began to speak of doing so.

Overview

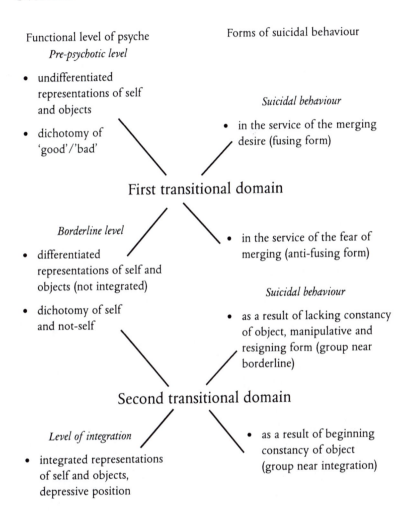

Figure 4. 1 Forms of suicidal behaviour between pre-psychotic and integrative levels

5

Countertransference

As a member of the caring professions one must expect to meet the usual countertransferential difficulties when dealing with patients showing suicidal behaviour. Partly this is because therapists and patients share two essential areas of conflict: difficulty in dealing with aggression; and difficulty with regulation of self-denigration (cf. Reimer 1981). The attendant conflicts are activated in the therapist by the patient and conversely. The therapist will therefore encounter difficulties that are not in the first place connected with the patient, but with his own psychic structure and choice of profession.

Doctors are more prone to suicide than other professional groups (Reimer 1981, 1982; Blachly, Disher and Roduner 1968). Their suicide rate is higher than average for the whole population, and they suffer more from depression and addictions. Amongst doctors, psychiatrists are endangered most. One must ask what is triggered in doctors when they meet in their patients what they have to fight off in themselves; i.e. when their own latent suicidal tendency (which defence mechanisms keep unconscious) tempts them because of their patients' suicidal behaviour.

Reimer (1981 p.2) describes how he as a psychiatrist examined a surgical out-patient because she had inflicted cuts on herself. The chief doctor of the clinic entered the room and roughly told the patient that people like her were not wanted there, and if she did attempt suicide she should do it efficiently. He was quite willing to tell her of a shop near the port where she could buy a proper rope, to hang herself at home in her attic.

Tabachnick (1961a, p.66) tells of a doctor, who after a successful revival, 'with undisguised hostility' remarked: 'Well, now you can go out and do it again.' Here we meet doctors who wish their patients dead. The Hippocratic oath seems not enough to protect them against their own latent tendencies, and one wonders why they are made to take it, except to ward off outside criticism.

Besides possibly explaining uncontrolled countertransferential reactions, these examples, at a concrete physical (and therefore unambiguous) level, point to the controversial relation between suicidal patient and doctor: the one injures himself, the other is to repair the deliberate damage. He is to do something that the patient can always destroy again, indeed will do so until reasons for it are revealed and better alternatives found. The patient does not merely show the therapist how near to death one can come if one wants to, but also that the patient's intention is the opposite of the therapist's. At least consciously, the patient wants death; the therapist consciously wants life.

The doctor's choice of profession seems particularly determined by fear of illness and death. Reimer (1981, p.23) has given convincing evidence for this; in his view, doctors are much afraid of incurable disease, death, impotence, dependence and helplessness. Doctors use their profession and its implied roles for protection against all this. Tabachnick (1961a, p.65) baldly asserts: 'As a matter of fact, it is often true that the choice of a healing profession represents a systemised reaction formation against the expression of sadistic impulses.'

Strong latent fear of death even before choosing? Defence against sadistic impulses as motive? Dealing with such dynamics by a jump forward into the professional domain where what is always at stake is life and death? The doctor appears as one who daily and openly acts to repel the death of others: it is that for which his studies prepare him. However, he is also someone who unconsciously thereby seeks to push back his own fear of ..ath and suicidal tendencies, and for that his studies do not prepare him. In the firm conviction of always being on the side of the patient as an ally in fighting illness and death, he ends his medical training and starts therapeutic work. Kreuzer-Haustein (1992, p.55), in her reflections on the reception of the death instinct in Freud's theory of culture, observes that doctors reject it, for a while abandoning the medical position and envisaging the disturbing possibility that life-preserving and healing powers ultimately fail. Wegehaupt (1981, p.146) points out that medical students resist medical psychology and psychotherapy because they fear that this might question their own decision to become doctors. Given such resistance, it is no wonder that the medical graduate is surprised and uncomprehending when he meets people in whom he cannot create the same attitude as to therapeutic goals that he had taken for granted; people who are prone to crises in which they consciously pursue the opposite course and seem to seek bodily harm or death.

A patient's suicidal behaviour hits a doctor (or member of the caring professions) where their conflicts are central to their personality. In the very field where he hoped he might best push back his own conflicts and fears of death, suicidal behaviour, impotence and helplessness, he meets them, and in a manner that can be identified with.

While countertransference has special difficulties and dangers, it offers matching opportunities too. Paula Heimann (1950, p.83) states that countertransfernce is the patient's creation and is part of his personality which supports our diagnostic and therapeutic reflections. The approach is often misread or at least exaggerated. In spite of her statement, countertransference is first an expression and part of the therapist's personality. Not everything that we experience with a patient allows direct inferences back to him, but relates above all to ourselves. This portion must be set apart and assessed. Only then can we turn to the patient and ask how what we find in ourselves is related to and fits in with what he contributes. Here we shall find that what we recognise as ours is not so different from what the patient has to work out with himself, which can offer profitable access to his psyche. This is what Heimann (p.81) means in calling countertransference an instrument for exploring the patient's unconscious. The therapist's conflicts are like a sounding board set vibrating by the whole gamut of the patient's interactive suicidal behaviour. A potential restriction can thus become an extension of perception. The fact of similar conflicts can sensitise the therapist to the matching aspect in his patient better than would otherwise be the case.

Countertransference has a range of very different meanings. Definitions run on a broad scale from very narrow to very wide (cf. Kernberg 1965; Sandler, Dare and Holder 1973).

Freud (1910, pp.104–115) tells us that he has noticed the countertransference the patient provokes in the doctor's unconscious; the doctor must recognise this in himself and master it.

This was often construed (see Nerenz 1985) as if Freud regarded countertransference as interfering, and only later authors had freed it from this role. The concept has indeed been developed much further, but he was right in his central assertion: the analyst must overcome his countertransference (and not suppress it).

In the course of time, it was increasingly emphasised that the analyst's countertransference cannot be understood without regard to psychic events in the patient and their setting, while conversely the patient's state and stories cannot be seen if isolated from the therapist's state and feelings. This has even led to the far-fetched view that countertransference comes before transference, which roughly means: as the therapist calls into the woods, so it echoes back.

Recognising transference and countertransference as mutually linked became necessary, particularly when psychoanalytic therapy turned more to pre-oedipal disorders. In dealing with such patients countertransferential reactions are often quite violent and one feels as if what goes on in one cannot issue from oneself, because it seems so strange. Some think that this strangeness is a good criterion for the presence and working of projective identification: what is strange to me must stem from another. This premature inference ignores that most of what is strange is in ourselves: we need not look outside to meet something strange. What is strangest and oddest we meet in our own unconscious; indeed, the strange that actually lies outside would seem less alien if we became better acquainted with our own strange aspects.

On the whole, one would do well to include in countertransference everything that one thinks and feels about the patient, both mentally and physically. Intense 'archaic' feelings (or affects) often gather in the body as primary source (a bodily feeling of disquiet, heavy limbs, precursors of anger in the stomach, a heavy pulse, goose pimples, headache etc.), before they form nameable affects and show up as such. This includes all feelings, impulses, fantasies, leanings to act and bodily reaction that one can find in oneself.

Two basic positions in dealing with suicidal patients

Feelings of countertransference in dealing with suicidal patients are manifold; here we are concerned with one sector from the total range of feelings and leanings to act that one usually finds in oneself. If one explores oneself for the feelings that one had, or now has, in dealing with suicidal patients, it will probably concern the following:

- worry about the patient and fear of him;
- mobilising aggressive impulses such as anger, hate and hostility;
- feelings of being at someone's mercy and under a spell;
- the feeling of being cornered by the patient and being manipulated;
- to getting hold of him in a counter-move, pushing him away and wanting to be rid of him;
- doing something to him in turn, e.g. locking him up or quietening him down by drugs;
- classifying as secondary all plans, thoughts and actions not relating to the patient;

- finally, guilt feelings.

Moreover, one will meet in oneself feelings of:

- resignation, helplessness and impotence;
- self-doubt and inadequacy;
- doubts as to one's own professional competence; even
- the feeling of not really being suitable for this profession.

At first glance this list looks extensive. However, if one tries to see some order in all these feelings, one notes that there are just two areas. The first is related more to the object; the second more to the self, the therapist's narcissism.

This division already makes it easier to diagnose counter-transference, but it is still an external criterion. If we take seriously the idea that we do not simply 'have' feelings, but always relate them to something or someone, so that we always must start from a subject interacting with an object, then in exploring our countertransference we must always include a hypothetical concern of the patient at the basis of this interaction. The patient is not simply hostile, nor feels simply desperate, trapped or ashamed past repair, but he is so with regard to someone. In therapy and transference he is so to us.

So, too, in countertransference we are not simply hostile, but are so to our patient; angry not as such, but at him and at ourselves. We become worried about him and are afraid for and of him. Or we are afraid of ourselves, e.g. of our own suicidal tendencies and aggression. (Much here depends on our specific personality.)

If we take seriously the fact that the patient in these states, now possibly aimed at us, reactivates old conflicts of early object experiences, we must further consider what sort of past relational partners of the patient we are to become here and now, and what the patient's intention is in stubbornly assigning this role to us. On this view, his suicidal behaviour no longer merely intensifies a biographical episode, in which we we might help from outside and show an escape (some see this as psychotherapeutic access), but it is a restaging of old conflictual object-experiences, for which he seeks a solution different from the old one, assigning to the therapist the role of the former partner in conflict.

Sometimes having countertransferential feelings in dealing with suicidal patients is regarded as something that we must master in ourselves, so that they do not become harmful. This is indeed important, but we must go further and not imagine that afterwards we are as it were internally free and cleansed and can turn to the patient's problems detached from ourselves. This would thwart the patient's intention and leave him alone, when one's aim was the opposite, namely to care for him. Rather, countertransference is more than merely our own problem: it is decisive in diagnosis and therapy. The role we are assigned by the patient, which we can determine by diagnosing countertransference, is often a key to what the patient has to master in himself. For instance, it assigns to us feelings of anger, hate and hostility, so that we can feel how things are with him. He conveys feelings of impotence, self-doubt, resignation, so that we know not only how he feels in such states, but can actually experience it. However, the patient not only assigns a role to us, in order that we can show him how we cope with it, but he also unconsciously conveys states that he could no longer perceive in himself, which we are to perceive on his behalf, formulate and bring into the therapeutic process and dialogue.

Countertransference of the manipulated object

On a visit the aim was to plan discharge. To the question of how things would continue outside and what she had planned, the patient shrugs her shoulders in mild disdain and replies: 'How should it go on? Probably I shall kill myself.'

A patient speaks of the great hopes he has placed on therapy. The clinic had been his last hope, but he could see now that that had been a mistake. He was surely too serious a case, beyond help. The only thing left was to kill himself. This was not meant as a reproach: on the contrary, he recognised the great trouble one had taken and wondered how one managed to put up with him for so long. Others would have given up much sooner; he could understand that therapy could help no further.

A patient who had often injured herself and tried to commit suicide, usually went to see the nursing staff shortly before the shift ended, to tell them that she could not put up with herself much longer. She can no longer guarantee her safety, and mentions it now because she has a suicide pact. She does not know whether she can carry it out. She rejects drugs, with the delay which this entails. She tells the nurse that her knife is stuck on the pin-board, but by tonight or tomorrow morning it might be stuck in herself. The duty nurse accompanies the patient to the latter's room and asks for the knife. The patient stands in front of her and silently looks into her face for a long time, and then without a word walks past her and leaves the room. Subsequently the nurse reports that she was so angry as not to be able to say anything to the patient and therefore felt helpless.

In these interactions the therapist is somehow powerless vis-à-vis his patient, who decides whether he wants to live or not. This state is real, but the problem of confronting the patient with his destructive behaviour has to do with specific conflicts of members of the caring professions. How experiencing the object can be manipulated in practice becomes clear in the following example:

A central topic in the analysis of Mr L (about 35 years old) was his fear of being at someone's mercy and powerless. He had tried to master this by attacks on the exploiting society which he held to have caused his 'deep and basic disorder'. In therapy, he experienced me as that society's agent who was not really interested in him, but merely aimed to turn him into a working member of that hated body. Progress in therapy was identical with submission and abandonment to it. In this phase he had become increasingly suicidal, and he made it plain that this was a crisis in his relation to me: I was not treating him properly, did not reach the 'core of his disorder'. His state was now worse than at the start of analysis. He had constantly hinted that my explanations rather missed the core. Now it was too late. He felt how the illness irrevocably advanced. He knew no way out but to kill himself. He could imagine the press having a field day. That would be the end of me, an idea he seemed to enjoy.

The patient, by his threat of imminent suicide, apparently wanted to get me into his grip, and I had to admit that he had partly succeeded. I reacted increasingly with fear and felt trapped and immobile, with guilt feelings and doubts as to my professional competence: my feelings had become the plaything of the patient. When he told me that he felt better, I was relieved, breathed again and was startled by feelings of gratitude. When his suicidal tendencies grew again, he seemed to tighten thumbscrews on me. At the same time I took fright at the sudden feelings of hating this and rejecting the patient for thus sadistically torturing me.

These are restagings of early interactions between mother and child: by withholding and unequally distributing its goods, society in the unconscious experience of the patient had become an overpowering mother figure, which at the same time wants to know everything about its citizens. In therapeutic interaction with me the patient had transferred the image of this figure on to me and saw me as an agent of society. He felt at the mercy of this agent, to whom in fantasy he had to surrender and tell everything. In the course of therapy conditions became reversed. The patient had become the controller and had stored in me a powerless part of myself feeling at his mercy, by activating in me a corresponding part of himself.

Another example:

On a visit a patient asked for weekend leave. We asked her what she meant to do and how she would spend the day. She shrugged her shoulders: 'What plans can I have in my state. It will no doubt be quite pointless. Perhaps I shall kill myself.' She added: 'If you do not let me go, I do not know what might not happen here.'

There seems no way out. Whatever you do is wrong, unless one moves to the next higher level and addresses the impasse that faces both patient and therapist.

Manipulative suicidal behaviour amounts to blackmail. It is like the ego taking the self hostage, to put pressure on the therapist. He must show the patient that the blackmail will not work. If the therapist gives in (e.g. by loosening restrictions on leave or stopping a medicine), the patient learns that the threat of self-destruction works, which might make him more uncertain still in dealing with his own destructiveness. If not even the therapist can resist, how can he be expected to?

Typical for the countertransferential state of object manipulation is the feeling of being trapped by the patient, as if being under an unbreakable spell, to be entangled with him in a rigid hold. One feels at his mercy, forced to be ever ready for him, dropping everything to offer an emergency session. By his suicidal behaviour, the patient has gained the upper hand.

Countertransferential guilt feelings in such cases can be similarly classified and understood. Inducing feelings of guilt can serve the securing of objects. People sometimes link up by guilt feelings in order not to have to let each other go. Likewise with mobilising aggressive impulses up to hatred. Maltsberger and Buie (1974) regard hate as made up of two components: aversion and sadism (respectively qualities that reject and bind objects). This seems to rest on what Abraham (1924, p.125) said about sadism. He distinguishes an early and a later stage of libido in the anal-sadistic phase: the earlier has tendencies hostile to objects, namely annihilation and loss; the later tends to hold and dominate. According to Maltsberger and Buie, in dealing with suicidal patients we must be prepared for our own feelings of hate, because such patients tend to provoke sadism in others. This important point cannot be overemphasised to therapists, who may well prefer to ignore such feelings. Who wants to admit that he has sadistic tendencies that can be mobilised against patients? Who wants to realise that prescribing extreme doses of psycho-pharmaceutic drugs, or clinical admission, may be not only consciously protective, but may be countertransferential hate, omitting the protective measures? In such tangles the supervision of the process of keeping different aspects of countertransference apart is vital. Maltsberger and Buie state that such a patient often can maintain links with objects only in sado-masochistic ways. This seems to me not to be so with suicidal patients in general, but plausible in the cases of manipulative securing of objects as here described. In a suicidal crisis caused by fearing loss of object a patient can see himself masochistically as a victim (since the other seems to reject him), but uses this role sadistically to manipulate a target person, e.g. a close relative or the therapist. In turn this can activate the therapist's masochism: if, unable to free himself, he stays too long in a subjectively painful therapeutic situation, this may express masochistic submission.

The feeling of being manipulated usually develops further and provokes anger, hate and hostility. These are of course reactions to feelings of impotence and being at the mercy of the patient, but they are a vital phase in the therapist–patient relation. They go on developing as far as the tendency to want to push the patient aside. This brings the therapeutic interaction to the decisive point with which the patient has always been familiar: the feeling of not being wanted and desired, and hence being discarded. To ensure that this development is not diverted from its therapeutic goal, we must allow our own hate and hostility towards the patient (cf. Winnicott 1949).

Countertransferential anger often arises from offending the therapist's narcissism. We saw Reimer's example of the surgeon angered by having to repair a patient's self-inflicted injuries. Here we note that the patient destroys not only himself, but also the doctor's work, namely the therapeutic measure, and so a part of the doctor who identifies himself with his work; that is the decisive point. The doctor can do nothing against the fact that a patient, whose suicidal self-injury had to be repaired, can always undo the repair. This is an essential part of countertransferential anger in members of the caring professions dealing with suicidal patients. As with the example of the surgeon, the patient can destroy the work of his therapist if he wants to, and he does, so long as he has to invert the original conditions of power (and lack of it in his experience) in order to stabilise his psychic balance.

The therapist must of his own initiative talk to his patient about such destruction. He in turn must explain why he cannot stand it if another feels responsible for, instead of indifferent to, him. For this concerns a part of him that seems insatiable for such an attitude, a part he must protect by countermeasures. To destroy the therapeutic work means to ward off an attack against this part.

The fear of countertransference can be fear of the patient and about him. A patient who has not quite given up his object, but fights for it and tries to bring it under control and make it independent of himself, will create fear in the object he manipulates. This is expressed, for example, in the fantasy of destroying reputation. This is fear of the patient. Fear about the patient is a sort of intensified care. Moreover, the therapist's fear can express the feeling of the patient leaving him.

All these feelings belong to a typical countertransferential state that occurs with a certain group of suicidal patients. My term for this is constellation of the manipulated object. The patient tries to secure the therapist as object by manipulative control. The motive for this can be the fear of being pushed aside. The patient is then convinced that one cares for him only in order to be rid of him as soon as possible. Or there is fear of being rejected because one is basically worthless. Generally, the patients are afraid to be at the therapist's mercy for good or ill, and therefore induce a similar state in him.

If the patient's biographical data point in a matching direction and the therapist diagnoses in himself this countertransferential constellation, he can fairly safely infer that the patient is threatened by fears (acute or chronic) of losing objects and that his concern is to secure objects. The therapist can then adapt his procedure and focus on these fears. Suicidal behaviour will not disappear, but it will acquire a function that makes sense to patient and therapist alike.

This constellation occurs when the relation of the patient who is suicidal (or potentially so) to his therapist nears a critical point. The patient's inner dynamics at this point are very complex and are only roughly described by 'fear of object-loss'. The interpersonal precursors involved in the development of such a state often involve narcissist crises triggered by offences (cf. Henseler 1984) and object losses, actual or threatened. To react, the patient can either resign and retreat, a dangerous development, or attack and manipulate. 'Attack' in a crisis, for a suicidal patient, is a means of trying to bring the object back under control. The patient seeks to secure objects, while the therapist feels manipulated.

Countertransference of the abandoned object

If vain efforts at securing an object by manipulation and changing it have stopped, or no efforts took place to start with, another state of countertransference appears. The therapist then feels that the patient no longer needs him, not because help is not needed but because it seems impossible. At first, this situation seems to be unlikely. Why should the therapist feel discarded, when it is the patient who imagines that people have given him up? Still, it is so: a feeling that we rightly surmise in the patient appears in the therapist. He feels that the patient no longer wants anything from him and internally passes by him, has given him up and is leaving him. The patient seems to leave, without further demands, and one sees him go. One seems to have no influence, no involvement, not guilty, just superfluous.

It is always amazing how well patients by their own behaviour can induce their own feelings in the therapist, and so convey their own condition, sometimes better than verbally. Because of the typical components of these countertransferential feelings (being abandoned linked with fear of object-loss in the therapist), we can here too speak of a specific countertransferential constellation: that of the abandoned object (Kind 1986), the second basic countertransferential constellation in dealing with suicidal patients (the first one being that of the manipulated object).

This constellation is less conspicuous and seems to try to escape the therapist's attention, so that one must actively look for it in oneself. The various component feelings are harder to grasp, less glaring and sometimes easy to miss. The patient has stopped (or never started) his manoeuvres of securing the object. In contrast with manipulative suicidal behaviour, these patients seem to make no demands on one. They report how pointless their lives have become and how indifferent they are to whether they live or not. It seems (and that is the really alarming thing) that there is no reproach against others or the therapist. The therapist feels less guilt, but rather helplessness and exclusion, having to witness events from which he is cut off without scope for influencing them. Also he has feelings of being trapped and under a spell. One does not feel the guilt of being entangled with the patient. One feels abandoned by him, he slides away. This can provoke the fear that one will really lose him. This is fear not of, but about, the patient. One feels that he has abandoned one. But there is a further fear that is less traceable and easier to overlook: the fear about the patient has added to it the therapist's fear of object-loss.

It is not now the patient who fears losing the object, as in the manipulative case, which would rouse him to a fight for preserving the object. Now it is the therapist who, when looking carefully into himself, feels this fear of object-loss (losing his patient). There is no need to stress that this is a very important state of countertransference. It tells us about a dangerous process: the patient's detachment from occupation. No longer is the patient afraid of object-loss, as perhaps he was at the start of his suicidal development. He seems to have come to terms consciously with this loss. Rather, this fear is now in the therapist. A last extreme form of this development occurs if the therapist gives up the patient, e.g. because he thinks that he is no longer in danger.

If one is treating several patients under suicidal threat, which is the rule in clinics, a quite definite difficulty arises for the therapist, nurses and carers: the team becomes exhausted by chronic overtaxing with suicidal patients. This can lead to misperceiving resignative suicidal behaviour. One is relieved if the exhausting manipulative cases diminish and perhaps overlooks the transition into the resignative form which is less interactional.

What strikes one in these patients is that there seems to be no connection between inner mood and outer events. They see no link between their condition and external events, at any rate if interpersonal relations are involved. This reminds one of patients with endogenous depression.

> A 40-year-old patient was admitted to the clinic because of grave depressive moods, self-reproach and the feeling of being worthless. She was convinced that she must really kill herself, as when she said: 'Nobody would miss me. My daughter would do better without me. She might even develop better.' She was good at introspection: when the crisis had faded she gave a subtle account of her state, but never referred to people with whom she was engaged. She did take part in joint activities with other patients, but attacks of self-denigration and contrition always seemed to come out of the blue. She said of herself: 'In such states the world is as if dead. Nothing can reach me. Last week it was so bad that I calmly and deliberately wanted to make an end of it.'

In therapeutic sessions, she seemed to me to be beyond my influence if in that state. Her obvious feelings of suffering showed that she needed (though perhaps did not desire) a change in her state, but she expected no help from the therapist or from anyone else. This contributed to the countertransferential feeling of being left standing or having been abandoned. I felt that she had left me, and I developed an image of a person swept off by the strong undertow of the receding tide; this seemed to point to the need to avoid anything that might cause interaction. The only self-worth she could see seemed to consist in ridding the world of herself. Besides, she had a latent fear of feeling dependent on someone. In therapy, she felt the danger of being understood by me, of becoming further engaged and then dependent on me. The desire to be understood provoked the deep fear of leaving herself undefended and then to be recognised as worthless. Friendliness and understanding became in her fantasy a grand act of merciful grace, which should be extended to her only if she felt unworthy, useless and contrite. However, if being understood was for her so close to being defenceless and therefore dangerous, it was clear that anything that might possibly help the therapist to understand her had to be avoided. 'Out of the blue', 'not triggered by others', 'not related to the therapist', these were protective measures against reliving an early mother–child interaction experienced as degrading. For the patient I was someone from whom nothing could be expected, and she thus repeated an aspect of the relation to her mother, who like me had to be forgotten because she was too disappointing.

What use is it to a patient to induce in the therapist feelings of hopelessness, being abandoned, and losing objects? The patient often has known these feelings for a long time, and now there is someone who also knows them, at least in tendency. This becomes a therapeutic gain only when the therapist transforms what he has learnt in this way. The patient had not provoked in me feelings of self-doubt or self-reproach: these were in herself. Rather, my fear of being abandoned had produced the impulse to want to hold on. That is the new element contributed by the therapist. This impulse was evidently a hint about an object that was too weakly developed in the patient. She had no adequate command of this protective inner object that she might have held and thereby expressed that she was worth holding. Such an object would have been better protection against her self-destructive tendencies. However, it was just by giving up active interactions that she had succeeded in transposing this aspect of the object into me or activating me, so that it was not lost, if we take the patient–therapist relation as a system.

Defence against countertransference

Someone not too familiar with the diagnosis of countertransference may find it odd that members of the caring professions can have hostile impulses towards their patients. Is not this precisely what they should not have? Not so. We all have hostile feelings. The question is rather how one should deal with them.

One reason for becoming aware of them, as always in counter-transference, is to prevent oneself from acting, and so protect the patient from our actions. Another reason is to show the patient that one can have such feelings without becoming destructive to oneself or others.

However, noticing such feelings often causes fright. Members of the caring professions are often convinced that feelings of anger, hate and hostility towards a patient should not exist. Reimer (1981) has shown that this frequently expresses one's own inner conflicts rather than a professional response.

What happens if these illicit feelings do exist? Here there is a wide range of defence mechanisms. The defence can be so complete that the therapist simply denies the patient's suicidal behaviour. One 'forgets' that on admission the patient spoke of his life having become pointless, of having previously made one or more suicide attempts, the last one only a few weeks before admission. This can result in psychotherapeutic activity being displaced to a less important area. The patient may help to further this so as to avoid painful and offending memories when discussing his suicidal behaviour. Mintz (1981) points out that the therapist's fear of a suicide attempt by the patient can prevent him from properly exploring the suicidal tendency, which in turn makes the patient feel more isolated again. In discussing case histories I have often observed that even in detailed interviews, the question of suicide was not raised, even when clear pointers to it existed. On the other hand, one can often observe that for the same reason (fear of the patient's suicidal tendency) the therapist explores the patient by controlled invasive questions. The patient can feel this as threat and persecution: he might therefore withdraw to escape from a pursuing object.

As mentioned above, Maltsberger and Buie (1974) regard hate as consisting of aversion and malice. It seems that the therapist's super-ego finds aversion easier to tolerate. It can show itself in the guise of caring duty: 'I am not pushing the patient aside, but putting him in more expert hands, e.g. in a clinic.' The result can be unfavourable to the patient–therapist relation. If the patient's main purpose is to maintain that relation, it can be understood that he must rely on the feelings alerted in his therapist, anger and hate included. Maltsberger and Buie point out that it is often hard to judge countertransference correctly, free from one's own neurotic components. One has to be aware of one's own tendency to push aside, which can masquerade as a duty to be responsible. Thus, when deciding to send someone to a closed ward, one needs to clarify whether this duty was unconsciously enlisted as a reaction, so as to conceal from oneself that the main motive was to get rid of the patient. On the other hand, such a measure is often necessary and a failure to act in time when the patient's self-destructive ways are beyond control could express an unconscious sadistic countertransferential feeling.

Since defence is unconscious, one does not notice it. At best one can infer it indirectly. Let me therefore list some typical signs indicating aggressive and hostile countertransferential feelings, as well as to feelings of self-doubt and inadequacy. Such feelings can exist in these cases:

- if one feels bored and inattentive in sessions with a patient who till a few days earlier made one feel powerless, helpless and angry because of his manipulative suicidal behaviour;

- if, when one feels utterly powerless, one imagines treating the patient with very high doses of neuroleptic drugs;

- if one is especially eager and engaged about the patient's welfare, relieves him of things that he could manage and renounces making him co-responsible;

- if one imagines that the patient kills himself to kill one's own reputation;
- if one feels threatened by the patient in some other way;
- if one lets oneself be tortured for a long period by the patient's suicidal behaviour;
- if one has become suicidal oneself.

Blind spots: the therapist's difficulties of countertransference in dealing with suicidal patients

> The analyst's personality bears on the course of treatment much more strongly than our theory allows. (Baudry 1991, p.917)

'Blind spots' are what psychoanalysts call their own unconscious conflicts in the setting of treatment, for such blind spots prevent them from perceiving certain conflicts in their patients. The analyst's perception is distorted. Some aspects of the patient are exaggerated while some are seen less clearly, and so the image is in certain areas formed by how the therapist deals with his own conflicts about the problem concerned. However, one need not have unsolved conflicts first in order to be prone to blind spots. The various character structures of therapists implies from the start a varied sensitivity for the patient's different aspects and problems (Baudry 1991, König 1992, Riemann 1959).

Blind spots result from the corresponding conflicts being unconscious. This makes one blind looking both inwards (what is unconscious one does not see) and outwards (what one has never seen, one cannot recognise) to the object. We implicitly start from the ego, which as the perceiver is partly blind. An unconscious conflict is marked by two opposed parties: unconscious instinctual impulses of the id pushing into the ego, and an ego that rejects them, by defensive activity that is also unconscious. Both parties are unconscious.

The ego's conscious part cannot see the content of its opponent id, nor its own defensive mechanisms. The conscious ego does not even know that such a conflict exists, and the conscious part of personality can only indirectly infer it. As to the list of signs that allow us to infer defence of countertransference in suicidal behaviour, the ego's conscious part deals with them as did astronomers who inferred the existence of Neptune indirectly from disturbances in the path of Uranus, at a time when telescopes were not yet strong enough to perceive the new planet directly. However, the comparison fails in one vital respect: astronomers then could not perceive what caused the disturbance; the bearer of an unconscious conflict is not allowed to. His conscious ego would be overtaxed. For instance, he must not perceive his hate, because that would contradict his ideal as carer, but he attains this limited but tolerable state by reaction formations.

Why does an unconscious conflict become a blind spot for perceiving corresponding processes in the other? After all, what we normally do not see in ourselves, we are only too ready to see in the other, even if it is not there at all and we see it into him, as it were. Such imported seeing is one reason for blindness. If I must not see my own fantasies about my importance (e.g. because I imagine I must accept and realise them, but then rightly feel that this must fail and I therefore behave with excessive modesty), I risk seeing conflicts of mine in my patients too and reacting to them inconsistently. I shall then, for example, misinterpret normal striving for reputation as an expression of megalomania, because I would do so in my own case. I would not regard it as expressing sound and sensible impulses but as the effect of conflict, and thereby limit the patient in his development. Conversely, I can use the patient as a substitute for living out of my own wishes and thereby overstimulate his ambitions, in order to experience in him what I dare not experience myself.

If I cannot perceive and assess something in myself reasonably free from conflict, I cannot react to it free from conflict in my patient. Freud (19¹⁰, p.108) points out that every psychoanalyst can go only as far as his own complexes and inner resistances permit.

However, it is not as if one must have 'solved' one's own conflicts (the phrase has become established but is not very appropriate) before one can help a patient. Searles (1966) in a different context speaks of fantasies of omnipotence that the point is not to solve them but to become aware of them. If unconscious conflict need not be solved, one should at least become largely aware of it, so that the ego can intervene if need be, anticipate rough passages in the process of therapy and so make dealing with them as free from harm as possible for the patient. This situation usually occurs where triggers are strong.

Even after analysis, any conflict will be only more or less solved and more or less conscious. How far it continues to be pathogenic depends on the ego's ability to render it conscious and on the intensity of the current triggering situation. Time and again, in treating suicidal patients we here meet triggers of high power. Even if for the rest one manages quite well:

- with one's own compulsion and the attendant fear of chaos and being at someone's mercy,
- with one's own depressive nature and the attendant tendency to feel guilt,
- with one's own narcissism and the attendant proneness to being offended,
- with the result of reactively repressed aggression and therefore limited confronting interventions

in suitably violent triggering situations these conflicts can become actual again.

Let me therefore consider some marks of character and describe how they can influence the handling of suicidal patients. For instance, the more compulsive therapist tends to judge differently from one who is more hysterical, depressive, schizoid or narcissist.

In a psychotherapeutic ward I had occasion to observe one and the same patient under a deputy, night service or change in teams. Sometimes different therapists regarded the severity of his symptoms very differently. This stands out in patients who are in crisis, thereby provoking fear in the therapist and requiring action. Since, depending on their own structure, therapists react differently to crises, we may expect that they diagnose 'suicidal behaviour' and 'suicidal crisis' differently, and deal with the patient according to their differing assessments.

Therapist's structure: hysterical

Therapists of predominantly hysterical structure need turbulence, otherwise they do not feel themselves enough. Therefore they tend to see crises where there are none, or not yet. They will diagnose suicidal crises more often than corresponds to a realistic assessment. They start more things than they can keep up with at length, and possibly interpret as suicidal (reacting to it with fear) the dynamics discovered in the patient, which might show itself in cutting or other self-inflicted injuries. As Riemann (1959, p.151) strikingly puts it, such a therapist gets into the position of Goethe's sorcerer's apprentice: he has activated so much that it threatens to overwhelm him and he suddenly becomes afraid and tries to ward off and reject, which can lead to a further crisis if the connections are not recognised.

In contrast with the compulsive therapist, who cannot let much develop at all and basically behaves in a controlling way, the hysterical therapist controls not at all, or only incidentally. He finds it hard to keep a uniform distance from all three parts of the structural model without favouring any, as Anna Freud (1936) demands. He tends to a special interest in the id, because he rightly expects that it will produce dynamics if mobilised. He lacks the patience for the usually arduous analysis of defence in the unconscious part of the ego. Anna Freud recommended an attitude in which the analyst attends equally to the three components (p.38). This uniform and impartial position, neutral as regards the three components, is difficult for the hysterical therapist. He is not like his more compulsive colleague who is more interested in dominating the id and in furthering the ego functions that serve to control. The hysterical therapist sets many things going and then has to try to bring them under control. This can lead to overcompensating measures, e.g. getting a patient admitted to a clinic prematurely.

Fear of suicidal behaviour can mislead the hysterical therapist into adopting an exploratory style that invades and controls. For instance, he might often and insistently ask the patient how he is and whether he has suicidal thoughts again, whether he feels safe, whether he has managed to avoid the motorway bridge and the like; behaviour that the patient possibly sees as threatening and persecuting and therefore furthers his moves towards retreat to escape from a pursuing object. Since hysterical therapists find it hard to rely on their feelings (they import feelings into a situation rather than observing them from it), they induce for instance situations causing concern, so that they may become active.

> A patient tended repeatedly to damage himself by cutting if he did not achieve his goals (including therapeutic ones in the ward) and therefore felt despised and rejected. He then felt even more worthless. This form of self-injury was better than the previous suicidal behaviour; but his therapist saw the cutting as dangerously suicidal and tended to ask after the patient's state more than was called for, renewing the suicide pact or seeking reassurance that in a crisis the patient would call. The patient felt hemmed in and reacted by retreating, which reinforced the therapist's initial assumption of suicidal behaviour and caused more intensive enquiries as to the patient's inner state.

In this way, circles of interaction can arise, in which patient and therapist mutually amplify their behaviour. If in fact a suicidal crisis occurs with the aim of securing an object, the hysterical therapist will react more to the crisis in himself and be less able to recognise the patient's wish and bring it under control. The compulsive therapist tends to underrate the crisis, the hysterical one underrates the need for control. Since the hysteric bears crises badly and tends to react to them dramatically, he will be less able to show how the patient's suicidal behaviour aims at securing his relation to the therapist.

Therapist's structure: compulsive

The more compulsive therapist is afraid of things getting away from him, but he mostly feels his fear less than the success of his control. The world controlled by him is the correct one. Uncontrollable domains are dangerous.

This therapist will therefore react rather touchily to his suicidal patient's attempt to bring him under control, and tend to enter a power struggle. The danger is that he will repress his own sadistic impulses or reactively keep them unconscious. This easily leads to acting. Particularly compulsive therapists can find it hard to deal with hate and sadism, and tend to split hate into aversion and malice, if we adopt the double structure of hate in Maltsberger and Buie (1974). Since aversion by the therapist's super-ego is usually preferred to malicious sadistic impulses, hate may act through rejection. A further concealment of the original impulse occurs if rejection masquerades as duty to care.

Since the compulsive therapist cannot tolerate tendencies to hem him in as object to be controlled and kept in check, he finds it hard to let countertransferential feelings of being manipulated develop. He soon reacts with countermeasures designed to free himself rather than help therapy. He is less able to tolerate impotence and so less ready to grasp that it is the patient who has shifted his own impotence onto the therapist by projective identification. In contrast with the depressive therapist (who tends to remain in the countertransferential state of being manipulated and tortured), the compulsive therapist is more likely to enter into a conflict, where the question is who will bring whom under control. Since he tends to use his method rather inflexibly, he will be less likely to vary his style in crises and will tend to seek salvation in perfecting his technique. In suicidal crises, he will possibly not be flexible enough as regards neutrality and anonymity, failing to see that by being anonymous he will cause a patient to experience a loss of object just occurring, so that suicidal behaviour can be his last chance to maintain a relation thus threatened. On this point, compulsive therapists resemble the beginner who sticks rigidly to method; the latter from a need to seek direction, the former from a need to control. His following a well-tried method can thus help to reinforce suicidal behaviour. The patient behaves in this way to force the therapist out of his anonymous reserve.

While Maltesberger and Buie regard the negative countertransferential feelings in the therapist as a reaction to a certain provocative behaviour of the patient, others (e.g. Tabachnick 1961a, 1961b) regard them more as due to the therapist's own problems. Tabachnick sees dealing with hostile and sadistic impulses as one of the hardest tasks for members of the caring professions. We saw his view that choosing to become a therapist is often a reaction to sadistic impulses. If a patient took the liberty (even against his wish) of acting on hostile and sadistic impulses, this would tempt the therapist to do likewise. But he is supposed to help the tempter, and this would make it harder to deal with his own hostility. The patient commits this hostile act with impunity, secretly envied by the therapist. Indeed, the patient usually gains positive attention. Here the therapist was in danger that his suppressed hostility might break through, showing itself in various open or concealed forms. Tabachnick (1961a, p.65) sees hostile and sadistic countertransferential feelings mainly as expressing the neurotic part of countertransference and not as a phenomenon unconsciously induced by the patient. 'In physicians and members of allied professions, it has been held that the choice of profession is significantly concerned with their conflicts over sadism and hostility.' By warding off the patient they can impose themselves nevertheless, and thereby 'forget' the patient's suicidal behaviour, leaving him uncontrolled in a dangerous state. Some authors (e.g. Bloom 1967, 1970; Tabachnick 1961a) see a decisive trigger for suicide in the rejection of the patient by the therapist under inadequate countertransferential diagnosis. (Andriola (1973, p.213) goes further and says that therapists under certain circumstances 'encourage patients to kill themselves.')

Therapist's structure: depressive

The depressive therapist wants to give in order to receive without having to demand. What he wants to get is a faithful patient who is not aggressive but gratefully appreciative of what is being given, for instance by staying.

The Roman legal formula *do ut des*, 'I give in order that you give', describes an important aspect of depressive structure: outward readiness to give conceals greed warded off.

Depressiveness makes it hard to demand without conflict, or rather to demand something for oneself. Others usually can. Demanding for oneself, if the depressive part of structure predominates, mostly means demanding too much. That is why the depressive therapist prefers to be given something without having to demand it. If 'it is more blessed to give than to receive' (Acts 20:35), this holds above all for the depressive part of structure.

To demand is always partly aggressive. One must want to have things and then take them. The depressive perhaps still feels that he wants things, but he does not want to have to take. That limits his initiatives. He must look for a way that turns active taking into passive receiving. For a strongly depressively structured therapist it is indeed at first more blessed to give than receive, because it allows this reversal.

However, he will never get full value. A basic unease will always disrupt his self-worth. He finds it hard to put up with feelings of dissatisfaction and wanting to have, and to see them as expressing his wishes to live and open out; he will condemn them as greedy and immodest, and push them back. However, the latent feelings are still there, and since he never had an opportunity to plumb their depth and never saw them as satisfiable and therefore finite, he must imagine them to be infinite. The result is guilt feelings. The capturing aggressive impulses that show up in spite of the *do ut des* re-emerge in the guise of guilt feelings, that is directed against the self. Aggressive behaviour provokes separation, this structure warns. That is why the depressive therapist will fear that the patient will break off the therapy if the therapist confronts him and is not permissive.

These conditions make it hard for the depressive therapist to deal with suicidal patients, where the problem always also includes guilt, aggression and separation. He will tend to see the fact of suicidal behaviour alone as a reproach, even if none is made explicitly. He will relate to it and regard it as justified. He is less likely to see it as a case of countertransference. Instead of reacting by interpreting, he will feel that he has given too little and will tend to make up for this.

Some patients accuse the therapist of looking on passively as they go to ruin. This hits the depressive therapist hardest, and he will be tempted to overcompensate, perhaps by making sessions longer, adding special ones or setting unusual times, to meet his guilt feelings. Often he rationalises that the patient is so disadvantaged that he has a quite realistic need to catch up. However, the therapist's extravagant giving can cause the patient's deep feeling of worthlessness and thus being unlovable to escape analysis. The depressive therapist gives from fear of negative transference, but he cannot avoid it anyway. However, when it shows up, he can react more by caring defensively and less by confronting and analysing. In a clinic one can readily observe how, through defensive caring, negative transference is expelled from the patient–therapist relation, and then attaches itself to another member of the team. In such cases one must clarify how far the patient's splitting tendencies were iatrogenically reinforced.

Guilt feelings in countertransference often play a major role in the treatment of suicidal patients. Sometimes we find a certain mechanism: the patient transfers onto the therapist a negative object-image. He feels that the therapist is not interested in him, being indifferent and not sufficiently caring, as the patient had experienced in relation to an early object. In some cases the patient hates the person seen in the therapist. The depressive therapist in turn will not recognise the transferential aspect because of his own tendency to have a bad self-image; he thus will perceive the patient more or less as real and correspondingly increase his therapeutic effort. In this way the hate and the therapeutic task in it escapes analysis. Hate impulses cause further feelings, amongst them guilt towards the therapist and fear of his vengeance. The mixture of hate and guilt can grow further if, on the basis of his readiness to suffer, the therapist allows the patient to torture and trap him, instead of bringing this out by confronting the patient and later resolving it by interpretation. If the therapist is too permissive and merely behaves so as to fend off his own aggressive feelings, the patient will begin to doubt whether the therapist is able to cope with him and his aggressions.

A further aspect is one's own suicidal behaviour. In a depressive therapist this is doubtless stronger, because of his inhibited aggression. In doctors, particularly psychiatrists, the risk of suicide is in any case high (Reimer 1981, 1982; Blachly *et al.* 1968). The causes are no doubt various. Bion made a suggestion of interest here (see Sandler 1987, cf. Ogden 1979): he sees one essential meaning of projective identification in the possibility of freeing oneself from a dangerous (or threatened) aspect of self or object and storing it in the other. Applied to suicidal patients, this leads to the idea of inducing suicidal behaviour in the therapist.

The reverse can be imagined too. Racker (1978, p.205) in discussing the analyst's masochism mentions that he might develop an 'unconscious negative countertransference in which the analyst shifts his sadistic inner object into the analysand'. This seems highly important. What goes on is really a projective identification with the usual roles of projector and recipient reversed: the analyst projects, and the patient has to tolerate what comes from the analyst.

Hence we may speak of inducible suicidal behaviour. The patient can induce it in the therapist and conversely, which suggests the notion of iatrogenic suicidal behaviour (cf. Andriola 1973), an idea that should be specially explored.

However, depressive structure involves not only a tendency to react to reproaches with stronger guilt feelings, but also to fend these off. Some people in situations where guilt would be appropriate cannot experience it, or hardly so, feeling aggressive impulses instead. To experience guilt is not negative, but an ability. One can speak of greater or lesser tolerance for guilt feelings. If it is low, guilt feelings may be replaced by a fleeting signal of anxiety, roughly meaning: 'Be on guard, the patient wants to make you feel guilty.' This can cause a preventive attack of the therapist on the patient: he defends himself against the patient dragging him into an area where he (the therapist) is to feel guilt feelings of his own. If he has problems there, he will not see this induction of guilt as an attempt by the patient to point him to an important topic, but as an attack against which he must defend himself. That makes it difficult for him to enter this area with the patient.

Projective identification is not a consciously controlled process of conveying. The patient will not bring up the topic of guilt feelings in words. This becomes conscious only when the recipient (the therapist, if projective identification issues from the patient) becomes aware of some feelings of his own. If he sees them as proceeding from a content conveyed by the patient, the unconscious message has succeeded, and further therapeutic steps can follow. If, however, he sees the content as aimed at his real self, then the process has become stuck half-way. The therapist did grasp the decisive content in himself, but did not recognise the meaning of the induction. This is a typical crossroad of therapy: either meaningful work continues or a tangle arises with stronger modes of conveying denoted as acting. Here the therapist, intending to promote structure, often points to the general conditions for therapy and tries to get the patient to commit himself to them, without recognising that the patient must attack and question these conditions. He must, because he needs the therapist's non-destructive prohibition of his acting. He needs that because, hitherto, prohibition always meant something destructive that hindered his development. In such settings, to relax general conditions, to allow the patient more latitude than before, merely postpones confrontation. The patient will seek a new boundary, since for his development he needs what occurs there between himself and the therapist.

If, however, the therapist's tolerance for guilt feelings is adequate, it is easier for the patient to lead him into this area, where he can then extend a certain therapeutic aim and work on it. The smaller this tolerance, the stronger the patient's interactive manoeuvres will have to be to convey the topic of guilt to the therapist. If the therapist fails to grasp the unconscious aim, a vicious circle arises in which reproach and attack alternate; the patient may then have no way other than his suicidal behaviour, to show the therapist his own failure, in short that he is guilty.

> A patient regarded a move of mine as wrong and accused me of thereby causing damage to her. If now she were to injure herself, it would be my fault. I reacted with irritation. Again she is trying to make me responsible for her, I thought. You must tell her that she is responsible for herself. When she asked me if I were annoyed, I confirmed this and said that I was irritated at her renewed intention to damage herself. However, this was only half the truth. At that moment I was really unable to tolerate the guilt feelings arising in me and was dealing with impulses to attack her as having produced them (to justify myself etc.). At this point I had left the therapeutic process, since I took as real and directed at me what was aimed at a transferential figure. Since I could not recognise that her unconscious aim was to arouse in me guilt feelings and an awareness of imperfection, so that she could make this area openly a topic for therapy, a spiral developed. She drove on, to the point of suicidal behaviour that could not be described as a threat. She took her own self hostage and threatened it, to force the therapist to enter a certain therapeutic field with her.

Therapist's structure: schizoid

The schizoid therapist has trouble finding what for him is the right balance between nearness and distance. His unconscious wish is to be close to others; in the end this is closer than his critical limit, so that he becomes afraid of merging with his object and has to react by seeking distance. In fixing his distance he therefore does not start primarily from what seems favourable to the patient, but from his own conflicts in this area. For the sake of caution he will choose a distance large enough for his ego to feel safe from opposite desires; larger than others who have fewer conflicts there.

On the basis of this behaviour towards his objects, the schizoid therapist will typically have trouble in two areas: in dealing with forms of suicidal behaviour concerning close links with the object; and in using the projective identification that selectively bursts through the boundary between self and object.

As to the former, he will find it hard to open out and work on fusing suicidal behaviour, since it resides in the field of his own conflicts and can activate them. The patient's wish to merge is tempting for this therapist, whose latent also wish is also to merge with the object. However, this object is suicidal. The schizoid therapist will therefore not readily allow this topic to come up. He runs the risk of seeking distance from the patient too soon, since a temporary identification would bring him dangerously close to merging desires that would destabilise his ego-boundaries. Perhaps he will emphasise the aggressive aspect of this form of suicidal behaviour, so that he may enter a field that meets his own desires of delimitation without having to leave the topic of suicide. This therapist will more easily handle manipulative aspects, although here, too, closeness to the object is essential. However, the point here is not a feared merging with the object, but securing it without touching the ego-boundaries, which for him is easier. A compulsive therapist would here react in a more touchy manner.

Therapist's structure: narcissistic

The therapist's narcissim is greatly stressed in psychoanalytic therapy, especially in dealing with suicidal patients. In a way, the therapist himself is the diagnostic and therapeutic tool. While in organic medicine the cause of failure is more easily separable from the therapist's person (lack of effective drugs or surgical procedures), in psychotherapy this is not so simple. The psychotherapist therefore tends to look in himself for the cause of failure, since he, rather than what he does, is part of the effect on the patient, or helps to develop such effects.

The narcissist therapist will be more sensitive than those of different dominant structure to these general conditions of psychoanalytic therapy. Confirming or idealising signals mean more to him and he therefore perceives them more clearly than would, for example, the compulsive therapist, who is more receptive to attempts at control, or the depressive therapist, who is more receptive to guilt.

The narcissist therapist sees himself as rather gifted and therefore as not having to plod as much. That is why whatever he does must succeed, preferably without much effort.

If he stresses that he can do quickly and economically what costs others much time and effort, he thereby tells himself that he is more powerful than others. For him, lengthy therapies are less the result of difficult and complex developments that need time if they are to succeed, than a hint that he cannot solve the problems quickly. Hence patients of narcissist therapists can be pressured to perform, and so develop guilt feelings because their progress in therapy do not match the therapist's expectations.

For any therapist, suicidal behaviour is a challenge to his own narcissism, since it is a classic situation of offence: his action fails. This particularly offends the narcissist therapist's expected ego-ideal, that whatever he does must succeed. He will therefore tend to deny the patient's suicidal behaviour. Maltsberger and Buie (1974) see in the therapist's narcissism one of the main difficulties in dealing with suicidal patients.

A further point arises: therapeutic efforts not only fail (this might happen with other patients too), but the suicidal patient actively destroys them. A patient who reopens a wound stitched up by the surgeon not only destroys part of himself, but the surgeon's work as well. Such a para-suicidal or suicidal act is an attack on therapy. His strong narcissist aspect will mislead the therapist to leave it at the offence, and not seek an underlying aim of the patient, perhaps by considering whether the patient too experiences the sort of denigrating and offending states as the therapist feels now; whether this is the patient's way of conveying it because he cannot put it into words; whether he wants to know how to cope with this without turning away from people, despising them and so isolating himself.

While the depressive therapist denies the patient's suicidal behaviour because he fears a loss of object, the compulsive because he fears his own destructive impulses being mobilised, the narcissist therapist denies suicidal behaviour because it attacks his feeling of self-worth.

Alongside this basic difficulty caused by narcissism, a more specific one is linked with integration. The better able the patient to form integrated images of self and object (i.e. the more realistic his perception of objects), the more readily he will take back his idealisations. Less narcissist therapists can recognise the progress this involves. The patient perceives his environment (the therapist included) more realistically and is therefore better able to find his way in it. The patients show that they have grown strong enough to discover bad features as well in the world (the therapist included). These external features are really there and no longer something inside projected outward. Even before, when bad things were mainly projections, the world was bad. As to that, nothing much has changed. However, the bad detected now serves to extend the ego, no longer to relieve it.

The narcissist therapist must react ambiguously to these discoveries in his person. For him, who mainly identifies with his ego-ideal and therefore has less feeling for the discrepancy between his real ego and his ideal, such discoveries mean a reduction of his worth. It offends him if the patient no longer sees on him clothes he never wore. However, the patient can only push ahead with the painful (and relieving) dismissals of his own illusions of magnitude, and so clear the path for integrating his own inflated self with his devalued one, if the therapist can do likewise.

6

Therapeutic Attitude

Principle of anonymity and abstinence, and fear of loss of object

> You always talk of my having this need and satisfying that; what I really want is a father. (Fairbairn 1946, p.64)

Neutrality, abstinence and anonymity, these three principles of the psychoanalytic attitude, are part of the general conditions under which the therapist contributes to the analytic process. He abstains from instinctual needs, both his own and the patient's. He is neutral towards the patient's ideas of values, convictions and goals; and anonymous towards his personal characteristics.

The controversy between Freud and Ferenczi on how strictly an analyst must abide by anonymity and abstinence in order to do successful work, independently of the patient's specific problems, we shall not go into here. This has been amply discussed, for example by Cremerius (1984) and Thoma (1981). However, we must note that if these principles are made absolute, one may look past the patient and miss specific ways of treating him given his structure. Cremerius therefore pleads for an operational use of abstinence rather than a rule-bound one (p.793).

Use of the abstinence–anonymity attitude should be tied to the specific task in hand. In patients with early disorders, the therapist will relate and attune it to their ability to have constant objects, which is one parameter in its use.

In borderline patients the main issue is not to further the transference of inner representations. Their conflicts have rather greater need of the interpersonal field than those in transference neuroses. We must start from the fact that the patient, without a sufficiently stable image of the other, is less able to keep absence apart from non-existence. When the therapist goes on leave, patients want to be able to imagine where he is, and their anxiety subsides as soon as they can locate him symbolically on a map. It might suffice to give the patient the resort's telephone number, which he can put on his shelf. I have not met an instance when it was used. In this way the so-far weak image of the therapist is activated, which is reassuring to the patient.

The therapist must therefore estimate how far to shed anonymity and show some aspects of himself when patients risk losing his image. If he refuses to consider this and sticks rigidly to the rule, patients who try to locate him and seek him in their own inner world of objects look in vain. A patient who has more reliably constant objects can fall back on the therapist's image even during the latter's absence. Some analysts infer from lack of object constancy that a patient is less able to agree to collaborate; in my experience, such an uncritical inference is not borne out by the facts. The working relation with borderline patients is often very good, and frequently permits more intensive work than with other patients. One might say that the relation is inconstant though the working behaviour is good: that is part of the problem on which therapeutic work turns. Of course, the inner world of borderline patients is peopled by images of others, too, the therapist included. But they are easily pushed into the void, because of lack of integration – namely when the therapist's behaviour disappoints the patient, of which mere absence is the simplest example.

With borderline patients, the analyst who expects transference under the strict rule will not get what he is after, namely a transferred aspect of self or object and scope to work with these projections as such. Instead, by sticking too rigidly to the principle of merely mirroring, he creates in his patient an idea of loss so acute that it overtaxes the patient. Since he does not show himself, he is not there, hence he does not exist. The therapist has not reckoned with this second step and the risk therefore is that he will misread what follows from this unacknowledged non-existence. How, then, will a patient, who is easily menaced by fear of object loss, react in such a setting? If he has not already given up hope for an attainable object, he will try to rediscover an object believed lost, and as it were recover it from under the magic hood of anonymity.

The next example comes from my early years of psychoanalytic work, when I still thought that one becomes a good analyst if one regards anonymity as a strict law and not as an important but flexible guideline, to be applied in terms of the particular analysis in hand. I emphasise this because the attitude seems typical of beginners looking for guidance. One wants to do the right thing and tries to hold the bow as the violin teacher had shown one. However, you can play music in various ways, and it will sound good when you have become attuned to your instrument. Even if your stance is classically correct, there is still the question of tone, how your attunement develops.

The case is that of the previously mentioned Mr L. In treatment sessions he and I became for some weeks involved in tangles in which he controlled and menaced me with his suicidal behaviour. The day after such a session I went to the clinic as usual for the daily ward discussion with the team. Suddenly we heard a shot. This was not completely unusual in the grounds (rural surroundings, hunters) and none of the team members gave it a thought. Not so with me this time: I suddenly thought that L had perhaps killed himself near my place of work and myself. I only half attended to the further discussion and could not shake off the thought of a possible suicide, but did not dare go out to look. Why did I not want this cleared up? If he had killed himself I should soon hear. If not, why not seek relief?

Only later did I dare answer this question: part of me wanted and needed the idea of his death. Without such ambivalence I would have gone down to find out what had caused the shot. Consciously I was afraid of a possible suicide and therefore did not want clarification. Unconsciously a contrary element may have been at play, namely the wish that at long last he had done it. Finding out might then have confirmed that this ambivalent but forbidden wish had been realised. Hence I must not try to find out. I spent the rest of the day in this state of fear and uncertainty. The patient was due to have his next session in the afternoon. In front of my room there was a hall where the patients waited. This one always came some minutes early, rolled himself a cigarette and smoked it. My door was old and warped, with a gap at the bottom which let through a wisp of quite pleasant smoke when he waited outside. I therefore did not need to open the door to see whether he was there or not. That afternoon I was anxious to see the smoke, for fear that he might stay away. When finally I smelt the familiar scent of tobacco I knew he was there. What a relief! I was grateful he was alive and smoking. He did not know what I had gone through these last hours, but indirectly he found out in subsequent sessions and weeks.

After I had seen what I myself had contributed to this development, I began to adopt a less cramped and rigid attitude to the mirroring principle of anonymity. I had been sparing in my interventions and in what I showed of myself; too sparing, in retrospect. The patient's fantasies in which he pulled me to pieces and devoured me frightened me off, and therefore I did not see then that this was his way of securing his relation with me. By his suicidal threats I felt pushed into the defensive; increasingly, he seemed to conquer the field for himself, leaving less room for me, my thoughts and fantasies and in the end my interventions. My impulse was to push the patient back to regain more space for my therapeutic activity.

The patient and I did not then grasp what was going on. In retrospect, it seems that he did not at first intend to control dangerous aspects of self and object transferred onto me, but rather wanted not to lose me so that he could do the control as a second step. One often hears it said that with suicidal patients one must place special value on the meaning of aggression, since that was a main problem in such cases. It is, but not always the primary one. Tabachnick (1961a) warns against addressing aggression and hostility too early, since that would heighten the strong guilt feelings present anyway, and this could lead to a wish for punishment. In the case history of a suicidal patient he writes: 'My interpretative work with her had mainly been in terms of pointing out her demanding and hostile attitudes. This had tended to increase her guilt and to make her feel a greater need for punishment' (p.576).

I realised that for a long time I had in a certain way treated this patient wrongly. In his experience I was not anonymous as I understood it, but I had subtracted myself. In the honest belief that I was obeying and using anonymity and abstinence, I had made myself unattainable. He had certainly transferred certain aspects of himself and his inner objects; however, my attitude had contributed nothing to clarify the relation further, but rather sharpened it. If he behaved towards me in a manipulative sadistic manner, he did so not merely to satisfy his own instincts, but with the connected goal of finding in me someone who would not be frightened or driven off by his behaviour but who would see it as his attempt to find someone who would understand him. Not that the therapist should now be consciously friendly and interested, by way of corrective emotional experience. That would be precisely wrong, because it would prevent these problematic sadistic relational parts of self and object from appearing in transference. In corrective emotional experience it is the therapist who decides on a suitable way of behaving that seems profitable at a given moment. By contrast we here mean a process in which the patient exerts pressure on the therapist's behaviour. The therapist can yield to this pressure: how far he will do so depends on his tolerance for temporary identification with the patient's aspects of self and object. Or he can defend himself against it. This patient is surely at first concerned to let me become existent and visible, so that on this basis he can work on his sadistic instinctual goals. He wanted to force me into an interpersonal relation, using every trick he knew.

Projective identification and projective identifiability

The second half of this heading is not commonly used: the first means unconscious and therefore involuntary identification of the therapist with what the patient projects. This concept has become the most discussed in clinical psychoanalytic literature. Meanwhile the definitions of projective identification have become so various that some authors (e.g. Meissner 1980) now urge that the concept be dropped. However, it still seems to me very helpful for understanding certain difficult situations in therapy and countertransference; provided we do not limit the definition to unidirectional processes (e.g. where the patient shifts his own psychic material on the therapist by projective identification). The patient can do this only if the therapist is flexible enough to let himself be projectively identified and will accept the material. The same sort of process takes place in the opposite direction, from therapist to patient. In this context we have already met the term 'iatrogenic suicidal behaviour' (cf. also Racker's hypothesis of shifting the analyst's inner sadistic objects onto the analysand).

This notion of bringing something of one's own to illuminate another, as if by invisible transfusion, gives quite a different look to the analytic process from that linked with the analyst as a linesman in a tennis match, who sits at the edge of the field, immune to rejection or attraction, calling out his interventions (Rangell, quoted by Cremerius 1982, p.502). Two mutually opposed pictures of psychoanalytic attitude? Immunity to rejection and attraction on one side (which presupposes an antibody in the analyst, to immunise him against the patient); and mutual influence between patient and therapist, with readiness to accept psychic material from the patient, which includes the attendant rejection or attraction, on the other? One might object that the comparison is inadmissible: you cannot compare a defence mechanism (projective identification) with a technical recommendation (the anonymous and abstinent linesman). True, but only formally so. It is certainly difficult to imagine that the concept of projective identification could have been developed from the attitude of a linesman. The idea that an analyst could see himself as a linesman is just as odd, when he sees part of his task as further developing feelings and fantasies induced in him by the patient, to offer them to him again for identification in a recycled and less destructive form.

However, the linesman comparison serves also to protect against the insight that the analyst, for his own relief, shifts unconscious material of his own on the patient. In the identity of a linesman such possibilities do not arise since no unconscious influences enter the court.

Perhaps the concept of projective identification has here helped to develop a countermovement in the psychoanalytic attitude. Its spread would then go back not only to a growing interest in patients with early disorders, but also to a need to replace the surgeon's unipolar mirroring by a more interactional understanding of the patient–therapist relation. Melanie Klein (1946) originally developed the concept of understanding for the patient who finds it hard to convey certain inner states: it is an extremely helpful concept. It can open a way where all else fails. Bion's concept of a 'container function' points to a certain therapeutic process. It consists in taking from the patient material that he can no longer bear without injury, e.g. destructive feelings. In a second step the therapist tries to give these feelings and fantasies a milder connotation, which Langs (1978) has called 'detoxification'. Greed, seen as destructive by the patient, can thus be interpreted to him as expressing his desire to live and fill emptiness. His fantasies of pulling the therapist to pieces to ingest them can express the desire not to lose him.

7

Defence in the Treatment Team

Collective defence

This term I owe to Kreische (1985). In psychotherapy with in-patients, to recognise in time that crises are in the offing, it is important to go beyond relations between two persons and to consider the dynamics of relations between the patient and the whole treatment team.

> One morning after the clinical conference the duty doctor reported the following incident to me: 'By the way, Mrs X (a patient in my ward) failed to return after a late leave. I asked in the ward and they reassured me: it had happened before several times, and she would then stay overnight with a friend or acquaintance.'

> This story caused me a sudden queasy feeling, a sort of inner kick, which I pushed aside as I left the conference. Later I realised that it was a sudden fear that she had committed suicide. The day before I had had a difficult talk with her from which I had left with a familiar dubious feeling, an inner signal full of meaning but in its essence unclear.

> The events then ran as follows: I went through the morning discussion with the team as usual. There too it was known that Mrs X had not yet come back, but not much importance was attached to it.

> In the discussion, other things were involved: times, daily planning, questions of organisation, current problems with patients. Only when that was over, after about 30 minutes, did we get back to Mrs X and now someone asked who had last spoken to her yesterday, what had been her plans, whether anything had happened to upset her at the time, etc.

The team members become more and more worried. Finally someone suggested that she might have made an attempt on her life. It would not be the first time – she had been admitted with several attempts in her case history. By the time this possibility was mentioned, it was about three-quarters of an hour after the duty doctor had reported the woman's absence. Hectic activity developed, all available telephones were used. In haste we tried to find out where she might be. Finally the rescue service found her in a room in a residential block, locked from within. She was in a highly intoxicated state, which after suitable measures she survived.

Later, nurses and carers reported that like me they had talked to the duty doctor and read the watchman's report, and had a curious feeling, perhaps a fleeting disquiet, but had not attached any further importance to it.

What had happened? The reports of the duty doctor and night watch set off a primary reaction in myself and the team, immediate but fleeting; we could not see its meaning and did not pursue the matter. Some time passed with routine work, until the feelings turned up again towards the end of the morning conference, now as disquiet and fear for the patient, and suitable actions followed.

I think that in the intervening period a powerful defensive process was afoot and prevented immediate conversion of the primary reaction into appropriate action. A set of feelings and impulses must have been at play that ego and super-ego sharply rejected.

What was up? Briefly consider the therapeutic phase before the suicide attempt: the patient had for some time been in a psychiatric clinic because of depression, treated with high doses of various drugs, and then transferred to us, because the diagnosis of endogenous depression no longer seemed plausible and neurotic factors as well as family tangles were now given more weight. Hence psychotherapy seemed indicated. After some weeks in the ward, the patient developed a certain mode of behaviour: she complained that nothing more could be done, no medicine and no form of psychotherapy could help her. Nevertheless, the clinic had been her last hope. She had come full of confidence and with the idea that she would be helped, but now it was clear that here too no-one could cope with her illness. She had often hinted that the way we went about therapy would certainly not help her. That was not a reproach, merely a bitter fact that she had to come to terms with. The only way out was to kill herself. Often she reported that she had just returned from the motorway bridge, where she had contemplated jumping off, but that this idea had now vanished again.

She considered herself to be incurable and therefore asked the team members to share this view. They did think that she was seriously ill, but not that there was no way out. In talks, she transmitted two opposite appeals: asking for confirmation that there was no hope left for her, and being freed from this hopeless condition. Attempts to instil hope in her made her react with a mixture of fear and protest. She seemed unable to bear hope: she was now told such things merely because her state was not really taken seriously, so that one could soon get rid of her. Preconsciously she may have seen something correctly here: she became increasingly hard to tolerate. In dealing with her, we felt ever more paralysed, helpless and impotent. Since her suicidal behaviour could always be unambiguously assessed, we had at times to consider putting her into a closed ward. If she was told of this, she protested and threatened that if we did this to her she would really kill herself. Whatever we did seemed to be wrong, a typical position when dealing with suicidal patients, possibly in the service of securing an object, a fact of which I was not then aware.

In this case, we readily recognise the object manipulation (of the team as a whole) and could no doubt deepen our understanding of the patient's world of inner images of object and self. However, let us use the example to clarify another aspect and ask how the team as a whole came to the dangerous denial of her suicidal behaviour.

We have seen various countertransferential feelings (especially anger, hate, hostility, impotence, being at someone's mercy) that very likely tend to trigger more or less vigorous defensive moves in the ego. By projective identification, such feelings can be taken as partly shifted onto the therapist, because the patient pressed by suicidal impulses can no longer handle them alone and needs an external bearer for relief. This would usually be an individual, for one experiences the content of identification in oneself. However, the bearer might be a group (cf. Heigl-Evers and Heigl 1983), for instance a team in a ward; but only if the team is willing and able to perceive and put up with such impulses. The ego and super-ego can always oppose seeing such contents. The ego can be overtaxed in its condenser function, as Balint once put it, and cannot take on such high pressures without suppressing or discharging them via action. Moreover, the super-ego can object in terms of its code and try to prevent such feelings from emerging, because they are incompatible with the ideals of the therapeutic profession.

Returning to the case in the example: between primary fleeting reaction and the start of action there was a phase in which we seemed to forget the patient. The countertransferential reactions with suicidal patients will on the whole have existed in the team as well. If so, we can regard the primary reaction to the message 'Mrs X has not come back yet' as a surface reaction to an underlying conflict that turns on hostility being difficult to bear and therefore to be kept away from the ego. This was done by denial (we did not pursue the matter) and rationalisation (Mrs X had stayed out several times before).

Let us further assume that our aggression had condensed into an unconscious fantasy, e.g. 'Let her then do away with herself!', so that the unconscious had formed a fantasy of removal. The super-ego will order the ego to fend off such a fantasy. What happens to such an impulse, which strives to become conscious but is stubbornly excluded? Usually this is the germ of symptom formation, namely a compromise between impulse and defence. At the group level what corresponds to the symptom is the formation of a psychosocial compromise, as studied and described by Heigl-Evers and Heigl (1979).

What does this mean for our case? If we assume that hostile impulses condense into an unconscious fantasy of removal and have taken shape, this fantasy should be discoverable as one element in the formation of the psychosocial compromise. This element is found in the progressive intoxication caused by the delay, which brought the patient closer to possible death.

The other side of compromise formation shows itself in the manifest behaviour of the team: they did what they felt they must, given their expressed notions of therapeutic activity. In the morning conference they discussed concerns of the ward and went through problems of patients. The compromise might be stated thus: 'We conscientiously do our psychotherapeutic work. We are free from blame.'

Splitting in the team: setting the psychic interior in the real clinical space

A single-minded team as in the example just mentioned is not typical, even if the purpose is defence. Here it resulted from the shared feeling, namely fear of an actual suicide. The unity of the defence crumbles if the shared feeling vanishes. Here the collective phase of defence lasted a good half-hour.

Much more often we find opposed points of view, sometimes even enmity. Some team sessions that discuss patients who do much staging in the clinic (often wrongly called 'acting'), are similar to court cases where an accused is discussed. Positions develop that remind one of the courtroom: the prosecutor on one side, the counsel for the defence on the other. The side of the public prosecutor defends the interests of the hospital and its personnel, of state and citizen as it were (limitation of time of stay, stress of ward staff, etc.). This side sees the patient more as causing difficulties and disturbing the running of the place. It is the side that the patient rejects in himself, which turns up again when the team overtly rejects him. At the same time the rejection induced in the team also produces the counterpart: one team member takes on the defence. Often it is the therapist, who must then be careful not to deny his negative countertransference, by which he grasps part of the patient. This danger exists when team members already grasp such negative feelings, and the therapist fears that the team lacks space for assessing positive countertransferential feelings. Just as in a courtroom, prosecution and defence discuss the points of view and arguments of the opposite side, but do not come to an understanding nor can identify with the opponent even if they wanted to; there is a sort of barrier between polarised team members preventing mutual empathy for fear of being deflected from their goal.

In team discussions about patients with borderline personality, who stage a lot in the clinic, thus causing much annoyance, work and fear, team members often become polarised in this way and try in vain to bring their points of view closer together. Why is this so hard? Because in such teams the patient's inner structure is represented too: his unreconciled aspects of self and objects. Both parties of the team are right, for both express the patient's inner truth: his rejected sides that make him feel bad and meriting expulsion and which via projection lead him to infer that others regard him so too, and his sides turned towards life and other people, which seek contact and led him to seek treatment.

The split of the team can thus be seen as expressing the patient's dual tendency. For a team, this stage marks a critical point in the patient's therapeutic process. The team's task is then to reduce the polarity being represented by bringing the oppositions closer together, and give back to the patient in integrated form what was earlier divided. This presupposes occupying a meta-level: one is not only a bearer of an aspect of the patient's self, but one must also be aware of this. The first step is mainly taken care of by the patient (by projective identification), the second is up to oneself.

In a team session the problem was a chronically suicidal patient who felt guilty about her mother's death, believing that she had committed suicide. Discharge had been considered several times, but had always been postponed because the patient was not well enough and again spoke often of possible suicide. Disquiet slowly spread in the team. 'What else can we do with her?' the question went. 'We are at the end of our tether; send her away, discharge her or send her to a country hospital', was the advice to the therapist. 'She has been here for almost a year, and if it has been useless till now, it will continue so in future.'

Actually some progress had been made, but the team members did not see it for the moment. The idea that one could not work with her had overshadowed the contrary experience and absorbed it. The chief physician, too, declared that the team was exhausted and things could not go on like this.

A state had arisen where people were no longer concerned to find out what was best for the patient. Such a shared task and goal of the team had now receded by regression of the team's working ego (of which more later).

Team members, with their more or less conflict-free ego domains, usually work together. There are conflicts and controversies, but the work is guided by the goal of identifying and applying those aspects that provoke controversy. Temporary identification with the other's opinion is common, as is taking on aspects that one had not seen in this way before, and modifying one's point of view. In this case, the contrary seemed to have happened. The single therapist of the patient had more and more slid into the role of a defence lawyer, and the team into that of the prosecutor. In discussions about patients the concern was no longer about developing a plan of treatment but was more reminiscent of the passing of a sentence. Discharge or transfer could no longer be seen as sensible indications that one could adopt or not, but evoked feelings as when a verdict is given. The defence wants to prevent such an announcement. The *co*-operation of the team seemed to have turned into an *anti*-operation. This new operating style of the team had the typical marks of borderline structure: a polarised black–white vision of irreconcilable contrasts, avoidance of mutual approach from fear of losing ground, i.e. active keeping apart of the contrasts, characteristic of splitting. Once this had become clearer to the team members, they were better able to abandon their polarised positions and assess matters more in terms of objective criteria.

Evidently what was true of the patient had emerged in the team. Either she saw herself as wholly bad, guilty and in the wrong and therefore meriting rejection, that aspect which re-emerged in the team's prosecuting role; or she felt in the right, worth defending and demanded therapy, a great deal of it, the aspect taken up by the defence.

However, we cannot infer that a team should take care not to get into such polar interactions on the grounds that they express a regression, which should be avoided. One might argue that a mature team always must move on a mature, ego-guided level of cooperation, but in fact the opposite is true: situations of polarisation are critical points in the work with borderline patients. They give us insight into inner events not easily obtained otherwise. The decisive step by which we profit from such sharpening of teamwork is indeed difficult: it requires the team to step down from the stage onto the floor of the auditorium to look at its product from there. It is the step from interaction to integration. In other words, team members must find their way back to conflict-free ego-activity and work through what has been produced in common, perhaps according to this formula: the two sides confronting each other must express matching events in the patient alongside possible real conflicts amongst themselves. Just as we avoid identification with the other's views in order to protect our own from being modified lest the other overpowers us, so it may well happen to the patient with his inner contrasts.

Regressive-progressive movement in the team during a cycle of projective identification

How are we to see these team processes, or rather the change in working level? In our example the team regressed from a mature cooperative level to one of borderline function. The point of the regression is that it produced material that helped in understanding the patient.

If we now apply the concept of projective identification to each of the procedures of the team, we see that it alternates between regressive and progressive working levels, running through the single steps of projective identification. This does not hold so clearly for every patient discussed in team sessions, but it is a tendency with difficult personality disorders, in which the mechanism of projective identification is strongly used.

Before applying this to our example, let us briefly look at the individual steps of projective identification, following the pattern of Ogden (1979). He divides it into four steps.

In the first, the patient projects certain aspects of his inner images of self and objects onto another person, who is called the recipient of the projection.

The second step consists in adapting the recipient to the projection. This is the curious process that the other is not only seen as corresponding to what is projected (this would still be projection), but is also to feel like that. This, as we saw, happens through interaction between the two partners (cf. König and Tischtau-Schröter 1982).

After that, the recipient in a third step is to develop further and make less noxious what has been induced (metabolisation, detoxification).

Only then can the patient, in a fourth step, identify himself with what has matured in the recipient. This completes the cycle of projective identification (Figure 7.1).

Applied to our example, the negative aspects of self and objects were projected on nurses and carers who more strongly represented the clinic as reality, and the positive aspects on the single therapist who looked after this patient, depending on the dominant transference triggers.

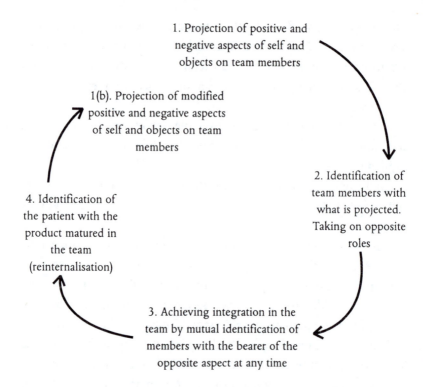

Figure 7.1 Sketch of the regressive-progressive movement of a team traversing the cycle of projective identification

In a second step the patient dealt with team members corresponding to her projections and got them to identify with the projected aspects (always depending on their own readiness). This is the situation in which team members in further sessions unwittingly enter a courtroom and find themselves in the roles of counsel for prosecution and defence. It is the regressively attained phase of collecting material, made possible by temporarily identifying with the features shaping the patient's structure. Transition to the third step is known to be difficult, for now the team is to progress from its intermediate borderline structure to the level of integration. This is often difficult unaided. At this point the team therefore needs supervision.

By its new approach to dealing with the patient, the team introduces the fourth step: the patient (if things go well) will be able to internalise part of the integrative material gathered from the team in its regressive-progressive cycle (e.g. the moderation of destruction in aggression).

If the third step fails, such patients sometimes remain a bugbear in the team's memory. After discharge of a patient from a team structure in phase three of the above cycle, one often must refrain from talking about this former patient. He must be forgotten. Perhaps, indeed, no-one will ask how he is. In extreme cases the team adopts the intermediate structure of 'one against all', the single therapist against the rest of the team, the hopeless case on one side and the hopeful one on the other; it is this polarisation that the patient recognises all too well in himself.

8

Classifying Suicidal Behaviour
by Types of Interaction

When I began to consider the theory of object relations in suicidal behaviour, it struck me that some suicidal patients occupied me and the
ward rather intensely, while others kept their trouble to themselves, as it
were, letting the therapist feel hardly more than that they were gradually withdrawing from him and the world. In a third group neither of
these situations seemed to happen. They behaved as if they were not
threatened and had quite a positive outlook. Their behaviour was
friendly, and if one suspected a critical development at all, one could
only conjecture it.

Three types of patient–therapist relation therefore occurred to me,
which earlier (Kind 1990) I called:

- rich in interaction, type I;
- poor in interaction, type II; and
- pseudo-stable, type III.

In classifying suicidal behaviour, we find these types again: the first corresponds to the manipulative form, the second to the resigned form.
The third type has not so far come up in the present volume.

It makes an essential difference whether a patient threatens with suicidal behaviour and thus makes his demands on the object interpersonally (type I), or whether withdrawing in resignation he no longer speaks
of his suicidal urge although he might continue to be strongly menaced
by it (type II), or finally whether he has internally resolved to kill him-

161

self, and after a desperate inner fight conveys an outer image of a calm and composed person who seems to be oriented by his own concerns and personal relations (type III).

Pöldinger (1982) sees three stages in suicidal development: consideration, ambivalence, decision. In the first, suicide is considered as a possible solution of the problem; the second is marked by appeals, cries for help and threats; the third by quietude, 'calm before the storm', to be taken as a sign of alarm. Pöldinger further recognises a change in the interactive behaviour of the suicidal patient: transition from a stage that is highly interactive to one that is less so and more intrapsychic. It is important to note such changes in suicidal interaction, particularly if the pressure on the therapist diminishes and he wrongly assumes that he can relax since the patient no longer uses the previous sorts of suicidal threat.

The rich in interaction form (type I)

This type of suicidal behaviour is the most common form of all. The patient tries to gain control over his therapist and it seems to be the fear of object loss that pushes him into this form of interaction. With the threatening idea that he will be abandoned, suicidal behaviour can help to generate a relation in which the suicidal subject has a hold over the object. By analysing his countertransference, the therapist can infer the patient's inner state. From a feeling that he cannot escape the patient, he can infer that the patient is afraid to lose his object. Further, the therapist's induced feelings of anger, hate, fear and guilt lead to the question whether the patient is about to be swamped by just those feelings and has shifted them to the therapist by projective identification.

The poor in interaction form (type II)

This form is not as often diagnosed as type I, perhaps because it is rarer, but this I rather doubt. It is more likely that it is harder to recognise, because it involves few interactions.

A patient came to me for therapy but could not say what she suffered from. She took tablets and drank, had made several attempts at suicide, got into dangerous situations from clumsiness and ignored feverish infections. Nobody seemed important to her, while she felt that she was not really important to anyone.

During therapy she remained suicidal for a long time, though this was hard to recognise and judge in the first phase of treatment. In her relation to me she hardly played a role, I could only conjecture her. At times I felt superfluous and that there was no link between us. (Winnicott (1982) once replied to the question when he regarded a patient as endangered: 'If someone comes and talks to you and in listening you feel that he bores you, then he is ill and needs psychiatric treatment' (p.5). One might add: what is decisive is to assess the countertransferential boredom as a symptom of an endangered relation.) In such phases I asked her to ring between sessions. Only later did it become clear that this request had been important and had protected her from suicidal actions. When she became more aware that she needed a reliable object, her suicidal behaviour took on a different quality. When gaps in therapy were imminent she not only felt suicidal, but made sure it was clear that such a pause was dangerous for her and that I could not responsibly impose one. Her suicidal behaviour had changed from type I to type II, a sign of favourable prognosis.

In contrast with type I, suicidal behaviour will hardly be used as an interactional means in type II. The patient does not use his suicidal behaviour as a threat; with luck the therapist might just perceive it. There is no engagement with the patient; on the contrary, he seems rather remote. There is no worry (as there is in type I) that one is neglecting the patient and spending too little time on him. More likely the therapist thinks he is no longer needed by the patient. He glides away, one cannot hold him. This countertransference seems to result from the inner void, resignation and apathy of the patient. If this lack of demand can be interpreted as a sign of alarm, both fear and worry arise in the therapist, and lead him to do something that the patient can no longer do alone: actively to look for a relation. While with type I, it is the patient who thinks he must hold the therapist lest he lose him, with type II this task is more explicitly the therapist's. He must try to hold the patient who might otherwise slide away. Here again projective identification can help us to understand: if a patient can no longer adequately protect, and care for, himself, there is a way of not losing these functions completely by temporarily shifting them on someone else.

This group of patients is without hope of creating and keeping an object relation. In contrast with type I, interpersonal behaviour directed to the object is therefore hardly noticeable. Nevertheless, these patients show clearly that they are unwell and threatened. They thereby give the therapist a signal that triggers worry and fear about them. This distinguishes type II from type III.

The pseudostable form (type III)

If an obvious suicidal case remains for some time in the interpersonal field with much disquiet and activity on the part of the therapeutic personnel, then a relaxation and calming down of the situation can be a dangerous sign. Psychiatrists noticed this long ago. The waning of suicidal behaviour without evident reason, the seeming solution of the problems of a patient who was previously depressively suicidal, must be taken as cause for alarm. From the perspective of libido, one can surmise that such a patient has completely abandoned outer and inner objects. His calm and equilibrium can then be his resolve to commit suicide. Consider the following case:

> A 25-year-old patient was admitted to a ward because he felt unsure of himself, inferior and fearful about asserting himself. In the first weeks of treatment he withdrew and barely allowed contact with him. An initial suspicion uttered by the therapeutic team that he might kill himself without prior hint later receded when his behaviour clearly changed. However, there was always someone on the team who was doubtful and worried about him. A

day or two before his suicide, this sceptic, too, was no longer doubtful. In the previous week, he seemed to have recovered better contact with fellow patients, sat in the common-room against his custom, and took part in conversations. Two days before his suicide he had a visit and, proudly confident, reported to the ward sister about emerging professional prospects. He was so convincing that even in this last bearer of doubt and worry concern for his stability vanished. The following morning he jumped from a bridge and died of grave injuries. He left no farewell letter, so that nobody ever knew what had moved him in his last days and hours. A proximate trigger event could not be found.

Another patient said: 'You get the feeling that nothing concerns you, the surroundings or people any longer. You are a bit merry, not euphoric, but somehow calm. If suicide has been decided, one feels relieved.' (In a review Musil says of Kafka's style: 'a friendly gentleness as in a suicide's hours between resolve and deed' (Corino 1988, p.215).)

Being hardly noticeable, this form of suicidal behaviour is amongst the most dangerous. In appearance it belongs to Pöldinger's (1982) third stage (decision). The ego no longer experiences the impulse as an alien urge that alerts contrary forces. Discussion of it is ended, its integration into the ego has occurred. The ego is no longer afraid of or disturbed by the impulse. In the course of this discussion, whose end finally leads to 'calm after the storm', efforts at still planning life can swiftly alter to preparations for suicide. Sometimes the ego rids itself of this tormenting ambivalence by a suicide resembling abduction.

In type III, the suicidal impulse has become ego-syntonic and has lost its impulsive character. Parallel to its integration into the ego, the capacity for pacts is gradually abolished, since the ego no longer need defend itself against a danger in which the therapist could be an ally. The suicidal behaviour has exchanged its threatening character for a relieving and stabilising one. Danger is no longer experienced.

The quietude, often going with feelings of relief and calmness, can be seen as instinctually expressing an exchange in occupation of lib: 'inous objects, accompanying a consecutive over-occupation of the self. A patient reports that in such a state she sees all people as small and miserable, blindly pursuing their petty concerns and keeping alive by paltry joys. She needed nobody, and nobody needed her.

If on the lowest level of a hierarchy of internalisation (Kernberg 1981) images of self and objects are internalised by a linked feeling, this axis between subject and object seems to be lacking here. The representation of the object remains, but the feelings leading to and animating it, however shaped (more libidinous or more aggressive), can no longer be activated.

This form of suicidal behaviour is hard to recognise. Hints are often derivable only from careful testing of the reasons the patient gives for his confidence and calmness. In countertransference one should therefore look for signs of doubt.

Table 8.1 Three forms of suicidal behaviour

	Type I	Type II	Type III
Form of suicidal behaviour	Rich in interaction	Poor in interaction	Pseudo-stable
State of the inner	threatened	given up	devalued, reactive occupation of the self-magnitude
Type of interaction	violent, struggle of patient with and for therapist	slight, in favourable case struggle of therapist for patient	seemingly serene
Counter-transference	feeling of being manipulated, impotence, hate, anger, guilt feelings, worry, fear	feeling of being superfluous and left standing, worry, fear	relief, at best doubt
Patient's main feeling	despair, anger of disappointment, vengeful feelings	apathy, resignation, inner emptiness	calmness, death as rational decision, 'calm after storm'
Feelings of being in danger oneself	present	begins to wane	absent
Character	dystonic	transition to syntonic	syntonic
Ability for antisuicide pact	mostly present	doubtful	absent
Degree of suicidal behaviour	serious but mostly manageable	threatening	hardly avoidable

Type I: The form rich in interaction is marked by the patient's struggle for his main reference person. In a therapeutic situation we find an interaction aiming at entanglement, in which the patient seeks object security. The term 'threat of suicide' really belongs here. The feeling of being manipulated, linked with feelings of impotence, can reactively provoke in the therapist anger and hate, and a tendency to push the patient away. Suicidal behaviour is largely ego-dystonic and is seen by the patient as endangering. Usually a suicide pact can be agreed and the matching therapeutic topics worked on.

Type II: It is characteristic of the form poor in interaction that the patient does not take on a relation to make up for resignedly abandoning an object. The therapist develops a tendency to seek out the patient and establish contact with him. The therapist can infer that the stronger such tendencies, the more the patient will relinquish his objects. Countertransferential feelings of being superfluous or left standing are not viewed on the surface as lack of interest and motivation in the patient, but as the experience of someone who feels superfluous and left standing and therefore is in danger of sinking into resignation and apathy.

Type III: One of the most dangerous forms of suicidal behaviour, the pseudo-stable form, exists when it has lost its interactional character (main criterion for type I) and no longer reveals itself in any way. This goes beyond retreat from occupation and the consequent paucity of interaction of type II. The patient can still maintain relations but people seem no longer to mean anything to him. One surmises that he has cut inner links with important reference persons and emotionally no longer lives genuinely amongst other people. Perhaps the patient has to choose this cloak of indifference as the only way of fighting off previous insults, disappointments and fears. In this situation doubt can be a possible last countertransferential hint to a life-threatening condition.

9

Antisuicide Pact

By antisuicide pact we mean agreement with the patient to deal with his suicidal thoughts and impulses (cf., for example, Modestin 1989; Wolfersdorf *et al.* 1984; Wedler and Kallenberg 1984).

Therapy usually develops according to the general conditions agreed; within these, collaboration arises and therapeutic topics unfold. An antisuicide pact, too, seems at first glance to be collaborative: the therapist conducts therapy under the terms of an agreement made with a patient hitherto beset by suicidal behaviour.

After that, things develop differently: the patient does not abide by the pact. Against its terms, he collects pills and buys razor blades, walks to the motorway or the railway station, cuts himself or upsets his potassium levels. If in a ward, he gives fellow patients a hint that he might kill himself and fails to return from late leave that evening. In his room, one finds blood-stained paper tissues. The staff and the therapist are alarmed, search messages are issued. One considers limiting leave and transfer to a closed ward. Then things calm down again for some days or weeks, but the slightest trigger is enough to start such scenes again.

Has the patient broken the pact as part of the working agreement, or must the working agreement be handled differently here?

While in fixing general conditions one does not as a rule talk about special symptoms, in an antisuicide pact a definite symptom becomes the core of the working agreement. The patient should no longer exploit in the old way a form of behaviour that fulfils important functions for him. Suicidal behaviour does serve the patient in assigning a certain

169

role to the other, but the antisuicide pact as experienced by the patient serves the therapist in keeping this role away from himself. The patient uses suicidal behaviour to give his therapist various functions:

- to regulate ego-boundaries by merging fantasies or distancing;
- to fight fear of object-loss by controlling the object;
- to attempt to change his negative image of the patient into a positive one, in order that the patient is not rejected: the therapist is to be shocked by the possible death of the patient and regret the part of guilt assigned to him. This presupposes that the therapist regards the patient's death as possible;
- via projective identification, to feel the patient's intolerable feelings of impotence, being at the mercy of someone, being threatened, being abandoned, doubting self-worth, in a way that conveys the aims and bodily goals described.

All this is put into question by an antisuicide pact. The patient is told: 'Suicidal ways are not sensible for you, but dangerous.' The latter is true, the former false.

However, the patient is not likely just to give up this scope for regulating, nor can he. He rebels against the pact, queries it and breaks it. This is not to say that one should not form such pacts. On the contrary, one should, for instance asking the patient to confirm that he will try to tell the therapist when a suicidal thought or impulse becomes so strong that he feels unable to control it.

However, we cannot start by assuming that this will have exorcised or delayed suicidal behaviour, so that the therapist can now turn to genuine therapeutic topics. The pact does not remove suicidal behaviour from therapy. On the contrary, it enters the more strongly, turning up in various functions.

While agreements are prerequisites for therapy, the antisuicide pact becomes their content. That is what makes actual the associated topics in the relation with the therapist:

- The therapist somehow comes too close to the patient through the pact, threatening his efforts at drawing boundaries and his autonomy.

- The therapist tries to bring under control the area where the patient feels threatened, and thereby makes actual the patient's feeling of being at his mercy and impotent.

In sum, the antisuicide pact hits the patient where his psychic functions are weak, not in conversation but in concrete negotiating interaction, and with luck in shared reflection on it. If the therapist concludes a pact with the patient, he tells him not to use suicidal behaviour as before, which brings to life all the themes involved in such behaviour. Central to the pact is not so much obeying it, as the struggle to obey it. In this debate between therapist and patient the central functions of suicidal behaviour show themselves and the attendant themes unfold. A therapist who decides to conclude an antisuicide pact with a patient should know that it will be broken. It must be broken so that suicidal behaviour can be discussed as a basic disorder in the patient–therapist relation. If no breaking of the pact is noticed, so that the therapist remains uninvolved, one wonders where the suicidal behaviour has gone. The seeming calm calls for doubt. Perhaps what we call suicidal behaviour happens at the moment to have no psychic function to take on. This would be the more favourable case, when therapy actually can turn to other less dramatic fields and their conflicts (boundaries between self and objects, desires for merging, fear of impotence and being at someone's mercy, feelings of being unwanted, etc.). However, perhaps suicidal behaviour has merely shifted to a different stage and shown itself in a different way, or has changed from type I (amenable to a pact) to the less interactive types II and III (no longer so). (In clinical psychotherapy split transference is readily observed: the transference of certain pathological object relations occurs not in the therapist; rather, they are realised in relations to other people, such as other patients. In the case of suicidal interactions, such extra-therapeutic forms of relation can be dangerous and difficult to deal with. It might be more restful not to be the target of one's patient's suicidal behaviour, but one then easily misses crises in the making.) In this situation the ability to form an antisuicide pact begins to wane. In type II a trace of it survives; in type III it has all but vanished.

Usually the therapist concluding an antisuicide pact is above all intent on protecting the patient: the pact has a protective function.

In the experience of the patient, that is not how it appears: he notices not so much that he is being protected, but that the therapist is being relieved, as if the latter is interested only in his own peace. That is why he asks the patient to call when suicidal behaviour becomes threatening. What he really wants is to keep responsibility at arm's length and leave it to the patient. This might be called the pact's relieving function for the therapist (while it is of course correct, and indeed essential, to show the patient that he is responsible for himself).

In my experience, therapist and patient come to assess these two functions of the pact both mutually and one-sidedly. The therapist sees mainly relief for the patient, the patient relief for the therapist. It is, however, important to mention and stress both aspects when fixing the terms of the pact, that one seeks to protect and relieve oneself as well.

> A patient admitted to a ward could not bear others being seriously concerned about him, an idea which he regarded as ridiculous.

> This patient was afraid of his strong desires for someone who would feel real concern for him. This desire and the attendant fear influenced the antisuicide pact, which the patient saw as hypocrisy on the part of the therapists, who thereby sought to relieve themselves of responsibility. They did not genuinely care how the patient was. The message of his therapist that self-relief was indeed the aim of the agreement, by involving the patient in responsibility, had a liberating effect on this patient. He laughed and said that he could somehow understand this.

The role of the means used for suicide

In wards as well as with out-patients, a frequent practice is to confiscate the means for suicide. If, via the pact, one requests that the patient should henceforth give up the suicidal mechanisms for mastering his crises and replace them by other less dangerous procedures, the demand on the ego is heightened by the surrender of the means. However, this cannot be achieved at once. It is a specious argument that the stopping of suicidal behaviour was not being demanded, so attendant functions could remain untouched. The pact is to achieve a measure of ego-dominance over suicidal behaviour and so to weaken its interactive power. The patient is urged to an inner working through areas where this is not yet possible interpersonally. If, moreover, one demands that he give up his tablets and razor blades, this may overtax him: the loss, without replacement, of scope for influence causes fear; the means for controlling the objects that enabled him to imagine merging or distance are taken from him.

Besides, only as long as he is in real danger can the patient feel sure that the therapist cares for him and is beginning to form a good image of him. However, he is in real danger only if he has his means of suicide. If he surrenders them, he must suppose that the therapist no longer regards the case as serious. Since for the patient it is always serious, he needs a serious situation, which he can see only with his means in hand.

> A patient, who came for treatment after trying to kill herself with an overdose of sleeping tablets, said that she wanted a new prescription for tablets since she could not sleep. She wanted to know what I thought of it. I become angry, since we had more than once talked about this and she knew my view: no tablets. I was unwilling to discuss the question further. Somewhat impatiently I asked why she was bringing this topic up again, since she knew my attitude. Fortunately, however, she does not give in and seems to wish to convey to me something that she herself is not yet aware of, and nor am I. Gradually it becomes possible to see the point of the tablets: the patient is never quite sure whether I recognise how bad

her state is at a given moment. If it is bad, she asks herself whether I can really imagine how she is, namely on the point of suicide. She feels that I would be convinced that she is in a bad state, and in danger, only if I knew that at home she had enough tablets for suicide.

At first I think (wrongly, as it turns out) that it was important to her to be able to threaten me, but the aspect of threat does not really meet the situation. Rather, the threat is to make plain to me how serious the situation is, conveying that only if I know that she has enough tablets for suicide will I see how serious her situation is. If she did not have the tablets I would say that things will be all right.

Having the means seems to have two functions for the patient:

1. It makes suicide possible and reassures the patient that this is a way out from a desolate situation. It brings the patient closer to death.

2. It has the opposite function, serving to point out to the therapist that the patient is in danger. The means thus have a clarifying function, aiming to start actions that help the patient to stay alive, maybe by getting the therapist to offer an extra session, prescribing a medicine or initiating clinical admission.

This does not mean that one leaves the patient his suicidal means without asking questions. On the contrary, one should ask him to surrender them; but one should be aware that he will not hand them over in every case, and this refusal may become the starting point of important therapeutic topics. Tablets and knives will be handed over (without prompt replacement) only if the questions mentioned above have been adequately discussed. This relates to the topic-generating function of the pact for the work between patient and therapist.

10

A Taboo
Death of a Patient

Mortality is inevitably linked with a doctor's work, whether his field be internal medicine, surgery or anything else. For the psychotherapist death seems to have a different meaning from that for members of organic medical fields. In general, psychotherapists probably think that death has nothing to do with their profession. Kulessa and Böhme (1980, p.630) reject this notion for psychiatry when they say that death at one's own hand could simply be called death in psychiatry. So too for psychotherapy.

This cause of death, typical for psychiatry and psychotherapy, is less openly discussed than causes and cases of death in organic medicine. Compared with people in organic medicine, those who work in psychotherapy are differently exposed to stresses on their regulation of self-worth; I surmise that this is linked with the special sort of effects in psychotherapy. In organic medicine, healing measures are more visible and testable, besides being more connected with technical factors.

In psychoanalytic psychotherapy there is no excludable third aspect. The therapist himself is the diagnostic and therapeutic instrument; for this, he must up to a point be able to 'instrumentalise', as Paula Heimann (1950) has called it. As against the predominant objective effects in medicine, here we have the subjective character of psychotherapy. This almost entails a different attitude to failed therapy and death. The psychotherapist will see failed therapy more as his own failure than medical doctors do. He attributes success and failure more to himself.

It is interesting that the term 'iatrogenic' always means something harmful. Pschyrembel (1977) sees iatrogenic illnesses as called forth by actions and statements of the doctor, as the word implies. Such a state, caused by the doctor, seems to be harmful, as a result for instance of clumsiness. What is not noxious, what heals, is not 'iatrogenic', and comes not directly from the doctor, but is only administered or initiated by him. Such modesty is not so simply available for the psychotherapist. Psychoanalytic psychotherapy is essentially iatrogenic, issuing from the therapist. That this can be not only helpful and progressive, but sometimes harmful too, is unavoidable but rarely discussed. Andriola (1973) speaks of 'possible iatrogenesis of suicide', as we have seen. The earlier mentioned notion of Racker (1978) runs in a similar direction, assuming a shift of the sadistic inner object into the analysand.

Suicide is a topic that we are oddly afraid to touch on. We feel this when, amongst acquaintances, we speak of someone who has survived a suicide attempt, or of someone who has not. He clearly suffered from something other than an illness about which one might calmly enquire, and he was in a different sort of danger than a person who had had a heart attack or a traffic accident.

A relative who has died from suicide makes us silent. While much is discussed at family feasts (other deceased persons included), he is not. Not from having been forgotten, but because the memory of him is so strong. It is as if one must not touch him.

Why is there is this embargo on discussing relatives, acquaintances and, in some measure, patients who have committed suicide? Freud (1912, p.43) gives a surprising answer: one who has violated a taboo becomes taboo himself, since he has the dangerous property of tempting others to follow his example. He arouses envy; why should he get away with what is forbidden to others? He is actually contagious, in as much as any example entices to imitation and must therefore be avoided.

In 'Totem and taboo', where this notion appears, Freud shows the close links between taboo and the formation of compulsive neurotic symptoms. This, he says, could equally be described as taboo illness. The compulsive patient puts a taboo on those areas, activities, objects and ideas that are directed to specially strong but forbidden desires.

A taboo thus involves two opposite forces: one towards realising a desire, and the other condemning it. If therefore we think we can see a zone of taboo in relation to suicide, we shall have to show the forbidden desire that imposes the taboo.

Many authors speak of taboo in connection with suicidal behaviour and suicide. Litman (1965, p.325) in his article 'When patients commit suicide' examines how the therapist works through a suicide. He interviewed 200 psychotherapists shortly after a patient had committed suicide and found clear barriers to talking about such an event: 'The question, "How do you feel about the death of your patient?" breaks taboos and intrudes into highly personal reactions.' According to Tabachnick (1961a) the doctor can experience the secretly envied act in his patient's suicide: the patient takes a liberty barred to the doctor, and it looks as if this echoes Freud, who a bare 50 years earlier saw taboo as the fighting off of dangerous impulses of envy: why should he get away with what is forbidden to others?

One reason for a taboo on suicide can thus be seen in the danger of infection, in the triggering of similar impulses (hitherto fended off) in the therapist and the relatives. However, if doctors, and particularly psychiatrists, are more prone to suicide than other professionals, the impulses and defensive effort must be correspondingly stronger.

In 'Totem and taboo' we find a further hint. Freud (1912, p.76) there studies relations between the quick and the dead and writes, referring to another author, that they culminate in the conviction that the dead in murderous mood drag the living after themselves. The dead kill; the skeleton as which death is pictured today shows that death is merely a dead person. The living felt safe from persecution by the dead only when they had established a separating water course between themselves and the dead.

Freud again confronts us with a finding difficult to swallow. If we represent death as a skeleton or a dead skull, we imagine that the threat of death comes from the domain of those already dead and not, as in fact, from ourselves. He gives an explanation for this inversion that is simple and of great importance: it is a projection of our own death wishes directed at the object, which it mirrors back to us. It is the well-known mechanism of inverting agents into victims, which relieves the subject.

Freud here points to a period in which touching a dead body, let alone uttering his name, was subject to a strict taboo. It was a matter of putting the greatest possible distance between oneself and the dead person. This was a protective measure, based on the dead relative becoming a dangerous and vengeful persecutor, even if one had done everything possible to keep him alive or ease his dying. Even mutual affection does not protect against the relative's hostility. This change of attitude that is attributed to the dead person is explained by Freud who says that no relation is without ambivalence. If such a relative dies, we react not only by a grieving externally visible part. There is also a part that was not dissatisfied with the death, and would have caused it if he had had the power (p.76). Further, such unconscious hostility hiding behind gentle love exists in almost all cases of intense feelings tied to a particular person; it is the classical prototype of ambivalence of human feelings (p.76).

Such statements are usually not welcome, especially if as psychotherapists we are dealing with suicidal behaviour and suicide, a region in which we become so easily entangled in events, indeed must allow this to some extent. Since we are here under strong pressure to assign to ourselves the blame for a patient's death, we will hardly like to examine our own hostility towards the patient; especially not if we expect to find it. Still, we cannot avoid it if we want to prevent its imposing itself in secret ways that escape our control.

Death wishes amongst and against people in general can be accepted. However, would it not go too far to assume that there are situations in which doctors and therapists, psychiatrists and psychoanalysts have death wishes against their patients and that a suicide could be seen as an unconscious fulfilment of such a wish? Since the choice of profession and membership of a professional group does not protect against being quite an ordinary person, with all conditions he is subject to, one will have to allow the above assumption. It does not go too far; at least not when one has ceased to regard man as primarily good and totally turned towards life, while the doctor is seen as only manifesting human qualities. Some people react indignantly if one regards man as bad too, and like to attribute everything bad to society. However, it does not seem to me reprehensible to reckon with a fair measure of badness in oneself: indeed, much is gained if one does not behave as one is.

A further reason for distance from the dead and therefore taboo on the question of suicide thus lies in our own ambivalence towards suicidal behaviour in our patients and, as part of that, in our hidden tendency to approve a suicide. With this tendency the suicidal behaviour of our patients confronts us always afresh, whether we like it or not. Nor can we do anything other than face this fact, so that we become more aware of our ambivalence in treating suicidal patients, in the hope that no excessive amount of hostility enters our treatments.

References

Abel, C. (1884) *Über den Gegensinn der Urworte.* (*On the Counter-Sense of Primitive Words.*) Leipzig: Wilhelm Friedrich Verlag.

Abelin, E.L. (1975) 'Some further observations and comments on the earliest role of the father'. *Int. J. Psychoanal. 56,* 293–302.

Abelin, E.L. (1986) Die Theorie der frühkindlichen Triangulation. Von der Psychologie zur Psychoanalyse. (The theory of early childhood triangulation. From Psychology to Psychoanalysis.) In J. Stork (ed) Das Vaterbild in Kontinuität und Wandlung. (The Image of the Father in Continuity and Change.) Stuttgart-Bad Canstatt: frommann-holzboog. pp.45–72.

Abraham, K. (1924) Versuch einer Entwicklungsgeschichte der Libido aufgrund der Psychoanalyse seelischer Störunge. (Attempt at a developmental History of the Libido based on the Psychoanalysis of Psychic disturbances.) In *Psychoanalytische Studien 1* (1971). Frankfurt a. M.: Fischer. pp.113–183.

Andriola, J. (1973) 'A note on the possible iatrogenesis of suicide'. *Psychiatry 36,* 213–218.

Balint, M. (1951) Über Liebe und Haß. (On Love and Hate.) In Urformer der Liebe (1969). (Primitive Forms of Love.) Frankfurt M.: Fischer. pp.133–149.

Balint, M. (1960) *Angstlust und Regression. Beitrag zur psychoanalytischen Typenlehre.* (*Anxiety Pleasure and Regression. Contribution to Psychoanalytic Typology.*) Stuttgart: Klett.

Baudry, F. (1991) The relevance of the analyst's character and attitudes to his work. *J. Amer. Psychonal. Assoc. 39,* 917–938.

Bergmann, M.S. (1966) The intrapsychic and communicative aspects of the dream. *Int. J. Psychoanal. 47,* 356–363.

Bernfeld, S. (1928/29) Selbstmord. (Suicide.) *Z. Psychoanal. Päd 3,* 355–364.

Biven, B.M. (1977) A violent solution. The role of skin in a severe adolescent regression. *Psychoanal. Study Child. 32,* 327–352.

Blachly, P.H., Disher, W. and Roduner, G. (1968) Suicide by physicians. *Bull. Suicidol.* 1–18.

Bloom, V. (1967) An analysis of suicide at a training center. *Amer. J. Psychiat. 123,* 918–925.

Bloom, V. (1970) Prevention of suicide. *Curr. Psychiatr. Ther. 10,* 105–109.

Buchholz, M.B. (1990) *Die Unbewußte Familie. Psychoanalytische Studien zur Familie in der Moderne.* (*The Unconscious Family. Psychoanalytic Studies of the Family in Modern Times.*) Berlin/Heidelberg: Springer.

Corino, K. (1988) *Musil, Leben under Werk in Bildern und Texten.* (*Musil, Life and Work in Pictures and Texts.*) Reinbeck, near Hamburg: Rowohlt.

Cremerius, J. (1982) Die Bedeutung des Dissidenten für die Psychoanalyse. (The significance of the dissident for psychoanalysis.) *Psyche 36*, 481–514.

Cremerius, J. (1984) Die psychoanalytische Abstinenzregel. Vom regelhaften zum operationalen Gebrauch. (The psychoanalytic rule of abstinence. From rule-like to operational use.) *Psyche 38*, 769–800.

Fairbairn, W.R.D. (1946) In P. Kutter (ed) (1982) *Psychologie der zwischenmenschlichen Beziehungen.* (*Psychology of Interpersonal Relations.*) Darmstadt: Wissenschaftliche Buchgesellschaft.

Federn, P. (1928/29) Selbstmordprophylaxe in der Analyse. (Prophylaxis against suicide in analysis.) *Z. Psychoanal. Päd. 3*, 379–389.

Fischer, P. (1986) Familienauftritte. Goethes Phantasiewelt und Konstruktion des Werther-Romans (Family Scenes, Goethe's Imaginary World and the construction of the Werther novel.) *Psyche 40*, 527–556.

Freud, A. (1936) Das Ich und die Abwehrmechanismen. (The ego and defence mechanisms.) In *Die Schriften der Anna Freud* (1980). (*The Writings of Anna Freud.*) Munich: Kindler.

Freud, S. (1910) Die zükunftigen Chaucen der psychoanalytischen Therapie. G.W. VIII.

Freud, S. (1912) Totem and Tabu. ('Totem and taboo.') G.W. IX.

Freud, S. (1916) Trauer and Melancholie. (Mourning and melancholia.) G.W. X.

Freud, S. (1920) Jenseits des Lustprinzips. (Beyond the pleasure principle.) G.W. XIII.

Freud, S. (1923) Das Ich and das Es. (The ego and the Id.) G.W. XIII.

Hartmann, H. (1972) *Ich-Psychologie. Studien zur Psychoanalytischen Theorie.* (*Ego Psychology. Studies on Psychoanalytic Theory.*) Stuttgart: Klett.

Heigl-Evers, A. and Heigl, F. (1979) Die psychosozialen Kompromißbildungen als Umschalstellen innerseelischer und zwischenmenschlicher Beziehungen. (The psycho-social formation of compromise as switching point of intra-psychic and interpersonal relations.) *Gruppenpsychother. Gruppendyn. 14*, 310–325.

Heigl-Evers, A. and Heigl, F. (1983) Die Projektive Identifizierung – einer der Entstehungsmechanismen psychosozialer Kompromißbildungen in Gruppen. (Projective Identification – one of the mechanisms for the formation of psychosocial compromises in groups.) *Gruppenpsychother. Gruppendyn. 18*, 316–327.

Heimann, P. (1950) On counter-transference. *Int. J. Psychoanal. 31*, 81–84.

Henseler, H. (1975) Suizidhandlung under dem Aspekt der psychoanalytischen Narzißmustheorie. (Suicidal behaviour as considered in the psychoanalytic theory of narcissism.) *Psyche 29*, 191–207.

Henseler, H. (1984) *Narzißtische Krisen. Zur Psychodynamik des Selbstmords.* (*Narcissistic Crises. On the Psychodynamics of Suicide.*) Opladen: Westdeutscher Verlag.

Henseler, H. and Reimer, C. (1981) *Selbstmordgefährdung. Zur Psychodynamik und Psychotherapie.* (*Threats of Suicide. Psychodynamics and Psychotherapy.*) Stuttgart-Bad Cannstatt: frommann-holzboog.

Hoffmeister, M. (1977) Michael Balints Beitrag zur Theorie und Technik der Psychoanalyse. (Michael Balint's contribution to the theory and technique of psychoanalysis.) Kindler, *Psychologie des XX Jahrhunderts.* (*Psychology of the 20th Century*). Vol. III (1982). Weinheim and Basel: Belz.

Jacobson, E. (1974) Depersonalisierung. (Depersonalisation.) *Psyche 28,* 193–220.

Kernberg, O. (1965) Notes on Countertransference. *J. Am. Psychoanal. Assoc. 13,* 38–56.

Kernberg, O. (1978) *Borderline-Stöungen und pathologischer Narzißmus.* (*Borderline Disturbances and Pathological Narcissism.*) Frankfurt a. M.: Suhrkamp.

Kernberg, O. (1981) *Objektbeziehungen und Praxis der Psychoanalyse.* (Object Relations and the Practice of Psychoanalysis.) Stuttgart: Klett-Cotta.

Kind, J. (1986) Manipuliertes und aufgegebenes Objekt. Zur Gegenübertragen bei suizidalen Patienten. (Manipulated and abandoned object. On countertransference in suicidal patients.) *Forum Psychoanal. 2,* 228–239.

Kind, J. (1988) Selbstobjekt Automat. (Self object as an automation.) *Forum Psychoanal. 4,* 116–138.

Kind, J. (1990) Zur Interaktionstypologie suzidalen Verhaltens. – On typology of interaction in suicidal behaviour.) *Nervenartzt 61,* 153–158.

Klein, M. (1946) Notes on some schizoid mechanisms. *Int. J. Psychoanal. 27,* 99–110.

Klein, M. (1957) *Envy and Gratitude.* London: Tavistock; New York: Basic Books.

Klemann, M. (1983) *Zur frükindlichen Erfahrung suizidaler Patienten.* (*On the Early Childhood Experience of Suicidal Patients.*) Peter Lang: Frankfurt a. M.: Suhrkamp.

Kohut, H. (1973) *Narziámus.* (*Narcissism.*) Frankfurt A.M: Suhrkamp.

Kohut, H. (1977) *Die Heilung des Selbst.* (*The Healing of the Self.*) Frankfurt a. M: Suhrkamp.

König, K. (1992) *Kleine psychoanalytische Charakterkunde.* (*A Brief Psychoanalytic Account of Character.*) Göttingen: Vandenhoeck u. Ruprecht.

König, K. and Tischtau-Schröter, R. (1982) Der interaktionelle Anteil der übertragung bei Partnerwahl and Partnerveränderung. (The part played by transference in choice and change of partners.) *Z. Psychosom. Med. und Psychoanal. 28,* 266–279.

Kreische, R. (1985) Kollektive Verleugnung und kollektive Ideologisierung als kombinierte Abwehform. (Collective denial and collective ideologising as a combined form of defence.) *Gruppenpsychother. Gruppendyn 20,* 356–387.

Kreuzer-Haustein, U. (1992) Schöngeister und Kleingeister. Klischeebildungen im Dialog zwischen 'Kulturtheoretikern' und 'Klinikern'. (Wit and pedant. The formation of stereotypes in dialogue between cultural theoreticians and clinicians.) *Forum Psychoanal. 8,* 47–62.

Kulessa, CH. and Böhme, K. (1980) Ursprung und Entwicklung der Selbstmord-vernütung in der deutschsprachigen Psychiatrie. (Origin and development of suicide prevention in German language psychiatry.) *Fortschr. Neurol. Psychiat. 48,* 629–642.

Langs, R. (1978) The adaptational-interactional dimension of countertransference. In R. Langs (ed) (1981) *Classics in Psychoanalytic Technique.* New York: Jason Aronson. pp.217–232.

Litman, R.E. (1965) When patients commit suicide. *Am. J. Psychother. 19,* 570–576.

Loewald, H.W. (1951) Ego and reality. *Int. J. Psychoanal. 32,* 10–18.

Mahler, M.S. (1979) *Symbiose und Individuation.* (*Symbiosis and Individuation.*) Vol.1: *Psychosen im frühen Kindesalter.* (*Psychosis in Early Childhood.*) Stuttgart: Klett-Cotta.

Maltsberger, J.T. and Buie, D.H. (1974) Countertransference hate in the treatment of suicidal patients. *Arch. Gen. Psychiat. 30,* 625–633.

McDougall, J. (1985) *Plödoyer für eine gewisse Anormalität.* (*A Plea for a Certain Abnormality.*) Frankfurt a.M: Suhrkamp.

Meier-Seethaler, C. (1990) Abshied von den Polartäts-Spekulationen in der Geschlechterpsychologie. (A farewell to speculation about polarity in gender psychology.) *Prax. Psychother. Psychosom. 35,* 130–139.

Meissner, W.W. (1977) Psychoanalytic notes on suicide. *Int. J. Psychoanal. Psychother. 6,* 415–447.

Meissner, W.W. (1980) A note on projective identification. *J. Am. Psychoanal. Assoc. 28,* 43–67.

Meyer, J.E. (ed) (1968) *Depersonalisation.* Darmstadt: Wissenschaftliche Buchgessellschaft.

Mintz, T. (1981) Clinical experience with suicidal adolescents. *Adolesc. Psychiatr. 9,* 493–496.

Modestin, J. (1989) Zur Psychotherapie der akuten Suizidalität. (On the psychotherapy of acute suicidal states.) *Psychother der Med. Psychol. 39,* 115–112.

Nerenz, K. (1985) Zu den Gegenübertragungskonzepten Freuds. (Freud's concepts of countertransference.) *Psyche 39,* 501–518.

Neumann, E. (1987) *Die große Mutter.* (*The Great Mother.*) Olten/Freiburg i. Br.: Walter.

Neun, H. and Dümpelmann, M. (1989) Depersonalisation. In M. Hirsch (ed) *Der eigene Körper als Objekt.* (*One's own Body as Object.*) Berlin: Springer.

Ogden, T. (1979) On projective identification. *Int. J. Psychoanal. 60,* 357–373.

Pöldinger, W. (1982) Erkennung und Beurteilung der Suizidalität. (Recognition and assessment of suicidal behaviour.) In C. Reimer (ed) (1982) *Suizid, Ergebnisee und Therapie.* (*Suicide, Results and Therapy.*) Berlin/Heidelberg/New York: Springer.

Pschyrembel (1977) *Kliniches Wörterbuch.* (*Clinical Dictionary.*) Berlin: De Gruyter.

Racker, H. (1978) Psychoanalytische Technik und der unbewußte Masochismus des Analytikers. (Psychoanalytic technique and the analyst's unconscious masochism.) In H. Racker (ed) (1978) *Übertragung und Gegenübertragung. Studien zur psychoanalytischen Technik.* (*Transference and Countertransference. Studies in Psychoanalytic Technique.*) Munich: Reinhardt. pp.202–208.

Reclams Lexikon der antiken Mythologie (1984) (*Lexicon of Ancient Mythology.*) Stuttgart: Reclam.

Reimer, C. (1981) Zur Problematik der Helfer-Suizidant-Beziehung. Empirische Befunde und ihre Deutung unter übertragungs- und Gegenübertragungsaspekten. (On problems in the relationship between helper and suicide. Empirical findings and their interpretation in terms of transference and countertransference.) In H. Henseler and C. Reimer (eds) (1981) *Selbstmordgefährdung.* (*Suicide Threats.*) Stuttgart-Bad Canstatt: fromannholzboog.

Reimer, C. (1982) Interaktionsprobleme mit Suizidenten. (Problems of interaction with suicides.) In C. Reimer (ed) (1982) *Suizid, Ergebnisse und Therapie.* (*Suicide, Results and Therapy.*) Berlin/Heidelberg/New York: Springer.

Reimer, CH. (1986) Risiken im Umgang mit suizidalen Krisen-Patienten. (Risks in dealing with patients in suicidal crisis.) *Prax. Psychother. Psychosom. 31,* 320–331.

Richman, J. (1978) Symbiosis, empathy, suicidal behaviours and the family. *Suicide Life Threat Behav. 8,* 139–149.

Riemann, F. (1959) Die Struktur des Therapeuten und ihre Auswirkung in der Praxis. (The therapist's structure and its results in practice.) *Psyche 13,* 150–159.

Ringel, E. (ed) (1969) *Selbstmordverhätung.* (*Suicide Prevention.*) Bern, Stuttgart, Vienna: Huber.

Rohde-Dachser, CH. (1979) *Das Borderline-Syndrom.* (*The Borderline Syndrome.*) Bern/Stuttgart/Vienna: Huber.

Rohde-Dachser, CH. (1986) Ringen um Empathie. (Struggle for empathy.) *Forum Psychoanal. 2,* 44–58.

Roshco, M. (1967) Perception, denial and depersonalisation. *J. Am. Psychoanal. Assoc. 15,* 243–260.

Rotmann, M. (1978) Über die Bedeutung des Vaters in der 'Widerannä herungs-Phase'. (The significance of the father in the 'renewed approach phase'.) *Psyche 32,* 1105–1147.

Sachsse, U. (1987) Selbstbesch ädigung als Selbstfürsorge. Zur interpersonalen und interpersonellen Psychodynamik schwerer Selbstbesch ädigungen der Haut. (Self injury as self care. On the intrapersonal and interpersonal psychodynamics of severe self injury of the skin.) *Forum Psychoanal. 3,* 51–70.

Sadger, J. (1929) Ein Beitrag zum Problem des Selbstmords. (A contribution to the problem of suicide.) *Z. Psychoanal. Päd. 3,* 423–426.

Sandler, J. (1987) *Projection, Identification, Projective Identification.* Madison: International Universities Press.

Sandler, J., Dare, CH. and Holder, A. (1973) *Die Grundbegriffe der psychoanalytischen Therapie.* (*Basic Concepts of Psychoanalytic Therapy.*) Stuttgart: Klett.

Searles, H.F. (1966) Feelings of guilt in the psychoanalyst. *Psychiatry 29,* 319–323.

Sperling, E. (1980) Suizid und familie. (Suicide and family.) *Gruppenpsychother. Gruppendyn. 16,* 24–34.

Spitz, R.A. (1973) *Die Entstehung der ersten Objektsbeziehungen.* (*The Rise of the First Object Relations.*) Stuttgart: Klett.

Stengel, E. (1952) Enquiries into attempted suicide. *Proc. R. Soc. Med.* 45, 17–24.

Stengel, E. (1961) Selbstmord und Selbstmordversuch. (Suicide and suicide attempts.) In H.W. Gruhle, R. Jung, W. Mayer-Gross and M. Müller (eds) *Psychiatrie der Gegenwart.* (Present-Day Psychiatry.) Vol. III. Berlin/ Göttingen/Heidelberg: Springer.

Tabachnik, N. (1961a) Countertransference crises in suicidal attempts. *Arch. Gen. Psychiat.* 4, 64–70.

Tabachnik, N. (1961b) Interpersonal relations in suicidal attempts. *Arch. Gen. Psychiat.* 4, 16–21.

Thomä, H. (1981) *Schriften zur Praxis der Psychoanalyse. Vom spiegelnden zum aktiven Analytiker.* (*Notes on the Practice of Psychoanalysis. From the Mirroring to the Active Analyst.*) Frankfurt a. M: Suhrkamp.

Verne, J. (1872) *Reise zum Mittelpunkt der Erde.* (*Journey to the Centre of the Earth.*) Zürich: Diogenes (1971).

Wedler, H. and Kallenberg, C. (1984) Kommunikationstheoretische Bemerkungen zum Umgang mit Suizidpatienten im Rahmem der somatischen Erstversorgung in der Klinik. (Remarks about the bearing of communication theory on dealing with suicidal patients in the context of emergency treatment in the clinic.) In V. Faust and M. Wolfersdorf (eds) *Suizidgefahr.* (*Danger of Suicide.*) Stuttgart: Hippokrates.

Wegehaupt, H. (1981) Umgang mit Abwehr gegen Psychologie und Psychotherapie bei Medizinstudenten unter besonderer Berücksichtigung ihres Krankheits-verständnisses. (Dealing with defence against psychology and psychotherapy in medical students with particular reference to their understanding of disease.) In H. Bach (ed) *Der Krankheitsbegriff in der Psychoanalyse.* (*The Concept of Disease in Psychoanalysis.*) Göttingen: Vandenhoeck and Ruprecht.

Willi, J. (1975) *Die Zweierbeziehung.* (*Dual Relation.*) Hamburg: Rowohlt.

Winnicott, D.W. (1949) Hate in the countertransference. *Int. J. Psychoanal.* 30, 69–74.

Winnicott, D.W. (1971) Objekterwendung und Identifizeirung. (Object use and identification.) In *Vom Spiel zur Kreativität.* (*From Play to Creativity.*) Stuttgart: Klett-Cotta. pp.101–110.

Winnicott, D.W. (1982) *Bruchstück einer Psychoanalyse.* (*Fragment of a Psychoanalysis.*) Stuttgart: Klett-Cotta.

Wolfersdorf, M., Metzger, R., Kopittke, W., Restle, H., Studemund, H., Straub, R., Witznick, G., Hole, G. and Faust, V. (1984) Hospitalisierte depressive Patienten und Suizidalität – Erfahrungen und praktische Hinweise zum Umgang mit stationären suizidalen Depressiven. (Depressive in-patients and suicidal behaviour – Experiences and practical hints on dealing with suicidal depressives in the ward.) In V. Faust and M. Wolfersdorf (eds) *Suizidgefahr.* (*Danger of Suicide.*) Stuttgart: Hippokrates.

Zagermann, P. (1988) *Eros and Thanatos.* Darmstadt: Wissenschaftliche Buchgesellschaft.

Subject Index

Author Index